IMAGES
of Rail

THE RISE AND FALL OF PENNSYLVANIA STATION

The splendor of the former Pennsylvania Station has been preserved forever in this ethereal image taken around 1948 by the renowned photographer Bedrich Grunzweig (1910–2009). The porters in uniforms shuffling through a long, cavernous drive represent elegance and luxury that no longer exists in rail travel today. The below-grade carriageway, one of two, allowed passengers immediate access to the station without disrupting traffic above. (Courtesy of the Bedrich Grunzweig Photo Archive.)

On the Cover: A family patiently waits with other passengers for departures in the monumental concourse of Pennsylvania Station. This iconic image from the early 1940s, amid World War II, reveals the importance of the station as both a center for public transport and a symbol of American strength through a major international crisis. Marjory Collins (1912–1985) preserved this image of American wartime life and several others for the Office of War Information. Although difficult to imagine at the time, the station and its concourse would be lost within two decades. (Courtesy of the US Farm Security Administration and Office of War Information Collection, LOC Prints and Photographs Division.)

IMAGES
of Rail

The Rise and Fall of Pennsylvania Station

Gregory Bilotto

ISBN 978-1-4671-0534-7

Published by Arcadia Publishing
Charleston, South Carolina

Printed in the United States of America

Library of Congress Control Number: 2020934618

For all general information, please contact Arcadia Publishing:
Telephone 843-853-2070
Fax 843-853-0044
E-mail sales@arcadiapublishing.com
For customer service and orders:
Toll-Free 1-888-313-2665

Visit us on the Internet at www.arcadiapublishing.com

"Men are what their mothers made them."

—The Conduct of Life
Ralph Waldo Emerson, 1860.

For my mother, Sandra. She has always offered constant help and support throughout my life and especially while completing this work. Much like Ralph Waldo Emerson, I am what my mother has made me.

Contents

ACKNOWLEDGMENTS

The author wishes to acknowledge several institutions and individuals for granting access to collections and permitting the use of specific images and material for this book. These include the copyrighted images *Pennsylvania Station* (1948) and *Penn Station Demolition* (1963), courtesy of the Bedrich Grunzweig Photo Archive; William Rutherford Mead portrait (1890s), courtesy of the Century Association; *Blue Morning* (1909), courtesy of the National Gallery of Art in Washington, DC; *Pennsylvania Station* (1907), courtesy of the Smith College Museum of Art; *Penn Station at War* (1943), courtesy of the Smithsonian American Art Museum; and many images of Pennsylvania Station (1960s), courtesy of Norman McGrath.

Additionally, the author expressly thanks several institutions and organizations for the use of entire image collections and other media, including the Avery Architectural and Fine Arts Library of Columbia University, Brooklyn Museum of Art, Empire State Development Corporation, New York Public Library (NYPL), Library of Congress (LOC) Prints and Photographs Division, National Museum of American History in Washington DC, and Wikimedia Commons.

Finally, the author offers thanks to the photographer Norman McGrath for sharing his personal experiences while photographing the destruction of Pennsylvania Station in the early 1960s, the many individuals and experts who have guided this research over the last two years, and Arcadia Publishing, along with Angel Prohaska, for her patience and ensuring that the project reached fruition.

INTRODUCTION

The thin gold veneer masking the pervasive corruption of the Gilded Age, the period from the American Civil War until World War I, was vividly illustrated in *The Gilded Age: A Tale of Today*. The 1873 work, written by Mark Twain (1835–1910) and Charles Dudley Warner (1829–1900), offers a satirical impression of corruption and greed characteristic of the era. For many, the days were long and hard. Agricultural and industrial labor was dangerous and offered limited rewards. For a few, the nights were glamorous, occupied by elegant dinner parties and card games that contributed to the waste and excess prevalent at the time. This dichotomy in living was reinforced by an enormous gap in wealth, allowing the privileged and rich corporations to strip the rights and safety of workers. During the twilight of the Gilded Age in 1910, Pennsylvania Station opened its doors, and electrified trains operated from New York to Long Island, Pennsylvania, and distant stations across the United States. Although an improvement in public transport that enabled direct commutes from newly developing Long Island and New Jersey suburbs and others farther afield, the project uprooted slum tenements that were the dwellings of many impoverished New Yorkers and immigrant families. Additionally, injured workers, and worse, those who perished during its construction, were neglected and denied recompense. The gilding described by Mark Twain and Charles Dudley Warner, a thin, hammered sheet of gold applied to wood or metal to conceal the lesser material underneath, exemplified the contradiction of the new Pennsylvania Station, a glittering project that was a manifestation of progress at the expense of the disadvantaged.

In tandem with the terrible misfortune of many during the Gilded Age, the United States, among other developed nations, was at the forefront of major innovations and industrial design, leading to the creation of the Edison incandescent light bulb, Otis electric elevator and "moving stairway" (escalator), Ford assembly line, and the Jenney skyscraper (Home Insurance Building). The development of American machinery and technology advanced so expeditiously that visiting delegates from other nations marveled at the progress. Even the emperor of Japan was impressed and subsequently purchased American firearms, including the Gatling gun, to transform his feudal army. Perhaps progress was more evident through the immediate expansion of the railways, spurred by the first transcontinental connection in 1869. The iron rails brought faster travel and connected countless cities and towns across the nation. American consumerism experienced rapid growth, and scores of families immigrated from abroad, mainly southern and eastern Europe and Ireland, to capitalize on these new opportunities. Pennsylvania Station emerged as the penultimate public project of this modernizing revolution, the ultimate was Grand Central Terminal in 1913. The station boasted a multi-tiered concourse, electrified rails, expansive waiting rooms, a myriad of amenities, and more importantly, the tunnel connections carved beneath the East River with improved tunneling shields. A novel British invention, the shields were enlarged for Pennsylvania Station and would set the standard for later projects.

During his 1867 sojourn, Mark Twain equated life in Gilded Age New York to a domed and steepled desert, where the individual wandered a solitary path of dollars and business despite living among a population of nearly a million. After the passage of the 1864 Banking Act, almost all national wealth was transferred to New York, which endures through the Federal Reserve System. The city would become synonymous with money through the banking, brokering, and manufacturing sectors. As a result, the value of real property between 1860 and 1870 doubled to $1 billion, and fabulously expensive dwellings and corporate skyscrapers were erected over the succeeding decades, including the Dorilton Apartments (1902) and the Singer Manufacturing Company Building (1908), both in the ever-popular Beaux-Arts style. New York's business and commerce only intensified, and eventually, entire neighborhoods were swallowed, trading religious buildings and private residences for offices and warehouses. Trinity Church with its cemetery at Wall Street was a rare survivor. Fashionable New Yorkers, many of whom called Fifth Avenue home, commissioned the most celebrated architects to design sumptuous mansions in the Beaux-Arts and Châteauesque styles, particularly the Vanderbilts. At these illustrious homes, balls and dinner parties, the most exclusive hosted by Caroline Astor (1830–1908), were arranged for the nouveau riche, comprised of financial and industrial titans who conspired to accumulate enormous wealth in underhanded deals. Meanwhile, the average New Yorker, likened to a "wage slave," was trapped in a perpetual cycle of meager-paying work to survive. Pennsylvania Station was born in this New York, possibly through gossip about the expanding railway business at one of the notorious Astor socials. Nevertheless, a protracted rivalry emerged between the New York Central and Hudson River Railroad (NYCHRR), founded by Cornelius Vanderbilt (1794–1877), and the Pennsylvania Railroad, directed by Alexander Cassatt (1839–1906), culminating in two opposing transport centers.

The destruction of Pennsylvania Station, although an avoidable tragedy, was premised on numerous factors, namely declining revenue, poor planning, shifting views on public transport, and the desire to construct a more financially lucrative entertainment complex. The once-luxurious station, built during the opulence of the Gilded Age, was relegated to an inferior status, a testament to its artificially inflated past. Its replacement, Madison Square Garden (1968), and the truncated railway station below, were themselves soon threatened with demolition during the Neo Gilded Age. An era of breakneck growth starting in the 1960s that continues today, the Neo Gilded Age is marked by an increasingly broad disparity in wealth since profits have been directed to a small minority. Vanity projects such as Pennsylvania Station and Madison Square Garden (1968) have proved financially unsustainable, prompting quick calls for their destruction. This cyclical process of superficial construction is wasteful and detrimental to the long-term vitality of New York, and disregards the anonymous sacrifices made by thousands of workers. Once built, the structures should fulfill their intended roles or be repurposed rather than demolished, following the revitalized Gare d'Orsay in Paris, transformed for public benefit into the Musée d'Orsay in the 1980s.

During a lecture by the architect Samuel White at the New York Public Library in 2009, the great-grandson of the famed Stanford White (1853–1906) from the firm McKim, Mead, and White, he lamented the loss of the unique architecture in the numerous Châteauesque Vanderbilt mansions that once lined Fifth Avenue. The razing of these fine homes was shameful, given that many could have been converted into libraries or schools for public use. More importantly, their loss, along with Pennsylvania Station, erased the social context and history that shaped their construction. Instead, products of the Gilded Age, emblematic of a corrupt and harrowing period in American history, should have been preserved as a reminder of a time that should not be repeated.

One

Monopolies, Rivalries, and Public Transport in the Gilded Age

Before the construction of its classical behemoth in Midtown Manhattan, the Pennsylvania Railroad was relegated to an inferior location on the opposite shore of the Hudson River in Jersey City, New Jersey. The Jersey City Station, known later as Exchange Place, along with other intermodal stations along the riverfront, enabled Pennsylvania Railroad passengers to reach Manhattan by embarking on ferry journeys across the river to piers in New York. Passengers could then travel by horse-drawn carriages or elevated lines to Upper and Lower Manhattan, an inconvenient and time-consuming process. The rival railway company, NYCHRR, maintained its monopoly over rail travel in Manhattan and hindered any efforts by competing companies to penetrate the New York market. Consequently, the Gilded Age competition that developed between these two corporate titans was the genesis for the construction of Pennsylvania Station, with its tunnels and bridge access (1904–1916), and Grand Central Terminal, along with numerous suburban railway stations (1903–1918).

Although these colossal railway centers improved transport and encouraged economic growth, both were representative of intense commercial and financial rivalries fueled by greed and excess typical of the Gilded Age. After all, Grand Central Terminal replaced Grand Central Station due to its perceived inferior size, even though the latter had been inaugurated only three years earlier in 1900, and Pennsylvania Station would suffer the wrecking ball within a few decades mostly because its enormous size required incalculable maintenance. The two structures should be understood as archetypal examples of Gilded Age construction and, in essence, fulfilled the vain wishes of their companies and owners. These voluminous French-styled structures, while architecturally significant, were economically unsustainable in the longer term. Pennsylvania Station was razed along with many other Gilded Age buildings, including the Grand Opera House (1868), Madison Square Garden (1890), and the Singer Manufacturing Company Building. Grand Central Terminal nearly suffered the same fate but received a reprieve and was spared in the 1960s.

This 1871 stereoscopic view of Grand Central Depot was completed in the same year by the notable cast-iron architect John Butler Snook (1815–1901) in the Second Empire style. Favored by Cornelius Vanderbilt and imported to New York, the style originated with the redesign of Paris by Baron George-Eugène Haussmann (1809–1891) under Emperor Napoléon III (1808–1873). It eventually faded as the classically inspired Beaux-Arts style increased in popularity. The two images showing the left-eye and right-eye views of the same scene produced the illusion of a three-dimensional image when viewed through a stereoscope. (Courtesy of the Robert N. Dennis Collection, NYPL Miriam and Ira D. Wallach Division of Art, Prints, and Photographs.)

Another stereoscopic view of Grand Central Depot from the early 1870s reveals an architectural design following the grand boulevards and stately buildings of Paris, especially the mansard roof typical of the Second Empire style. Constructed at Forty-Second Street, it became the centerpiece of the Vanderbilt railway monopoly and led to the eventual development of Midtown Manhattan. (Courtesy of the Robert N. Dennis Collection, NYPL Miriam and Ira D. Wallach Division of Art, Prints, and Photographs.)

The wrought-iron train shed designed by the engineer Robert Griffith Hatfield (1815–1879), modeled after the contemporary Crystal Palace in London, can be seen in this 1870s stereoscopic view. The 90-foot-high shed, with its 530-foot vault, formed from Howe trusses, was painted in brilliant colors and then gilt. It was illuminated at night by 12 chandeliers and the six-foot-high emblazoned names of Cornelius Vanderbilt, the president, and William Henry Vanderbilt (1821–1885), the treasurer. (Courtesy of the Robert N. Dennis Collection, NYPL Miriam and Ira D. Wallach Division of Art, Prints, and Photographs.)

Mathew Brady (1822–1896), made famous for his Civil War images, captured Cornelius Vanderbilt in this daguerreotype portrait, which was a costly early photographic process developed by Frenchman Louis-Jacques-Mandé Daguerre (1787–1851) in 1839. The Vanderbilt family, traced to an indentured servant who immigrated to America from the Netherlands, settled in New Amsterdam during the late 17th century. Cornelius Vanderbilt, a descendant living in Richmond County, became exceptionally wealthy after founding the Staten Island Ferry service, selling it, and forming the NYCHRR monopoly. (Courtesy of the Daguerreotype Collection, LOC Prints and Photographs Division.)

The Vanderbilt wealth grew exponentially and was reflected in the lavish and highly ornate mansions that once occupied prestigious Fifth Avenue addresses. This 1897 image taken by Benjamin Falk (1853–1925) shows the home of William Kissam Vanderbilt (1849–1920). Designed by École des Beaux-Arts–trained architect Richard Morris Hunt (1827–1895) in the Châteauesque style, it was located at 660 Fifth Avenue between Fifty-Second and Fifty-Third Streets but was razed in 1926. French architectural styles were popular during the Gilded Age for both commercial and residential buildings. (Courtesy of the Miscellaneous Photo Collection, LOC Prints and Photographs Division.)

The 1883 Châteauesque style home of Cornelius Vanderbilt II (1843–1899) was the largest private residence ever constructed in New York, a record that stands today. Designed by the architects Richard Morris Hunt and George Browne Post (1837–1913)—the latter trained in the Beaux-Arts style by the former—and decorated by the French firm Jules Allard et Fils, it was situated at 1 West Fifty-Seventh Street and Fifth Avenue. In the late 1920s, it was demolished for the Bergdorf Goodman department store. (Courtesy of the Detroit Publishing Company Collection, LOC Prints and Photographs Division.)

William Henry Jackson (1843–1942) captured this image of Grand Central Station in 1900, the newly enlarged and modernized replacement of Grand Central Depot. The station, designed by the architect Bradford Lee Gilbert (1853–1911), erased the Second Empire style popular with Cornelius Vanderbilt in favor of the Classical Revival style. The grandeur of the station was short-lived, and construction of its replacement began in 1903. (Courtesy of the Detroit Publishing Company Collection, LOC Prints and Photographs Division.)

The main waiting room for Grand Central Station, designed by Samuel Huckel Jr. (1858–1917), can be seen in this 1904 image. The oversized waiting area included rows of hardwood benches, globe-shaped lamps, and a high ceiling outlined with marquee lighting, all typical of Gilded Age opulence. (Courtesy of the Detroit Publishing Company Collection, LOC Prints and Photographs Division.)

This 1920s postcard features the Jersey City Station, or Exchange Place, built by the Pennsylvania Railroad. It was redesigned by the engineer Charles Conrad Schneider (1843–1916) between 1889 and 1892, which included the vast train shed. Interestingly, the postcard highlights the Colgate Clock at left, adjacent to the Pennsylvania Railroad administration building, at center. (Courtesy of Wikimedia Commons.)

This image of the Jersey City Station waiting room from the 1890s or early 1900s offers an extremely rare glimpse of passenger facilities along the Pennsylvania Railroad. Although lacking the opulence of its contemporary, Grand Central Station, the waiting room contained popular Gilded Age decoration, including ornate hardwood seating, globe-shaped lamps, chandeliers, and abundant fenestration. It was the globe-shaped lamps, and their gas lighting, that Edith Wharton remembered in her 1920 novel *The Age of Innocence*. It remains one of the few surviving descriptions of this station. (Courtesy of Gregory Bilotto.)

After the American Civil War, Charles Conrad Schneider immigrated to America from Germany and commenced work on several civil engineering projects that included a redesign of the Jersey City Station. His inspiration for the station can be linked to European railway architecture, especially in Germany. The influences can be seen in this early 1900s real-photo postcard of Frankfurt Central Station. (Courtesy of Gregory Bilotto.)

William Henry Jackson captured the central span of the Washington Bridge (1888) in this 1890 image. Charles Conrad Schneider and Wilhelm Hildenbrand (1843–1908) designed the 2,375-foot bridge over the Harlem River before work had commenced on the Jersey City Station. Training in steel arch fabrication by the former, who had worked to design the Queensboro Bridge as well, undoubtedly helped him to win the Pennsylvania Railroad contract. (Courtesy of the Detroit Publishing Company Collection, LOC Prints and Photographs Division.)

After trains arrived at the Jersey City Station, ferries operated by the Pennsylvania Railroad transported passengers across the Hudson River to New York. This image of the *New Brunswick* was taken during a smooth passage in 1905. For passengers, these crossings compounded an already arduous railway journey that could be complicated further by rough water or winter ice. (Courtesy of the Detroit Publishing Company Collection, LOC Prints and Photographs Division.)

Another vessel, *Chicago*, also ferried Pennsylvania Railroad passengers across the Hudson River to New York. In this 1904 stereoscopic view, it was noted by the photographer that morning rush passengers would have traveled up to 30 miles from within central New Jersey. The railway expansion stimulated suburban development, and the ever-increasing need for a direct rail connection to New York can be evidenced by the filled double-decker ferry. (Courtesy of the Underwood and Underwood Collection, LOC Prints and Photographs Division.)

In a later stereoscopic view from 1918, taken from the precipice of a Manhattan newspaper high-rise with city hall below, ferries navigate the Hudson River between New York and New Jersey. The ferry service remained after tunnels to Pennsylvania Station opened in 1910, but could not match the ease and speed of direct rail travel into New York. (Courtesy of the Keystone View Company Collection, LOC Prints and Photographs Division.)

Before Pennsylvania Station, railway passengers traveling between New York and New Jersey utilized the Jersey City Station and the Cortlandt Street ferry slip connection seen in this 1909 stereoscopic view. The central high-rise in the distance is the Singer Manufacturing Company Building (1908). Once the world's tallest building, the Gilded Age relic was unfortunately razed in 1968. (Courtesy of the Stereo-Travel Company Collection, LOC Prints and Photographs Division.)

This early 1900s stereoscopic view of busy West Street in New York reveals a mix of commercial interests and passenger travel. Pennsylvania Railroad passengers would have encountered these exact scenes of organized chaos with hordes of horse-drawn carriages and wagons and even the occasional automobile while transiting New York. (Courtesy of the Keystone View Company Collection, LOC Prints and Photographs Division.)

The cacophony of sounds and foul smells had become even worse for railway passengers by the time of this photograph of West Street during a railway strike in August 1916. Through the commercial bustle, Pennsylvania Railroad Freight Terminal, a hub for passengers traveling to the Jersey City Station, can be seen at far left. (Courtesy of the Bain News Service Collection, LOC Prints and Photographs Division.)

This rare view from the motorman's cab along the elevated Ninth Avenue Line, taken between 1914 and 1915, reveals a final travel option for Pennsylvania Railroad passengers. Upon arrival at one of three ferry slips in New York (Battery Place, Morris Street, and Cortlandt-Desbrosses Streets), travelers could elect to ride the Ninth Avenue Line. (Courtesy of the Bain News Service Collection, LOC Prints and Photographs Division.)

A second view of the elevated Ninth Avenue Line was captured between 1914 and 1915, while electrified trains passed at the Fourteenth Street Station. Pennsylvania Railroad passengers would have accessed similar stations at Cortlandt and Desbrosses Streets. The line continued until operations ceased in 1940, when many of the stations were razed. (Courtesy of the Bain News Service Collection, LOC Prints and Photographs Division.)

The Colgate Company erected a series of manufacturing buildings during the 1890s and early 1900s, and an octagonal clock was installed at the apex. Although the 1924 clock was modeled after the company's famous and now discontinued octagonal soap, it soon became a landmark associated with the Jersey City Station. The buildings were flattened in the 1980s after this image was taken. (Courtesy of the Historic American Buildings Survey, LOC Prints and Photographs Division.)

The Jersey City Station was demolished in 1963, and with the later loss of the Colgate Company buildings, the land remained vacant. In the early 2000s, Exchange Place was built up with high-rises, including the Goldman Sachs Tower designed by César Pelli (1926–2019) between 2001 and 2004 in the Contemporary Modern style. The Colgate Clock, now adjacent to the tower and visible at lower right, remains one of the last vestiges from the past. (Courtesy of Wikimedia Commons.)

Two

THE CONSTRUCTION OF PENNSYLVANIA STATION

The construction of Pennsylvania Station in Midtown Manhattan was an impressive engineering feat, and its architecture was a testament to neoclassicism in the Beaux-Arts style. Although the station has been lost, a sense of space and power can still be imagined through its two surviving sources of architectural inspiration. The first, Gare d'Orsay, completed in Paris during 1900 for the Universal Exhibition held in the same year and later repurposed as the Musée d'Orsay in the 1980s, was the design impetus for Pennsylvania Station. It represented the latest in railway design and engineering, which the French had perfected. The station also became synonymous with the Beaux-Arts style, and was elevated on the world stage during the exhibition. When Alexander Cassatt and his French-trained architects, especially Charles McKim (1847–1909), visited the station in 1900, they were undoubtedly awestruck by its splendor and magnificence. Even today, as an art museum, with its elaborately coffered ceiling and ornate decoration, its grandeur has not diminished. It should not be surprising that many of its elements were reproduced in Pennsylvania Station. The second, the ancient Roman Baths of Caracalla, constructed outside Rome and accessible now as an archaeological park, had a significant influence on the design of Pennsylvania Station's general waiting room. Alexander Cassatt and Charles McKim toured the site during the pinnacle of Western appreciation and, in certain instances, appropriation of the classical world. A visit to the baths today instills the same monumentality, which remains unmatched in contemporary classical architecture or even modern examples.

Incredibly, Pennsylvania Station commanded more opulence and exceeded the size of either structure, but beneath the glamor of the Gilded Age station was the misery that confronted thousands of people. These included scores of displaced immigrant families and impoverished New Yorkers in the tenement slums of Midtown Manhattan and the workers constructing the mammoth station and its tunnels. Although property owners were compensated financially, the poorer tenants were overlooked and cast aside, while tunnel workers toiled in appalling and unsafe conditions. The Tenderloin neighborhood, the site of the new station, was named by a New York police officer referring to the high volume of bribes that enabled him to eat beef tenderloin for supper. This corruption, along with the poverty of its many residents, almost assured that their rights would be violated. In one example, an unexploded dynamite charge, left from days earlier during foundation blasting, suddenly detonated and hurled rocks into shops, houses, and people in the street. An elderly woman was struck while hanging laundry, and a baby was nearly crushed when rock penetrated the family dining room.

Perhaps the most beautiful example of the Beaux-Arts style was the Petit Palais, constructed by Charles-Louis Girault (1851–1932) for the 1900 Paris Universal Exposition. The intricate structure presented this French style to the world, then at the zenith of popularity, with its classical columns, capitals, urns, elaborate balustrades and dentilled cornices, dramatic sculptures, multiple balconies, and projecting oculi. (Photograph by Gregory Bilotto.)

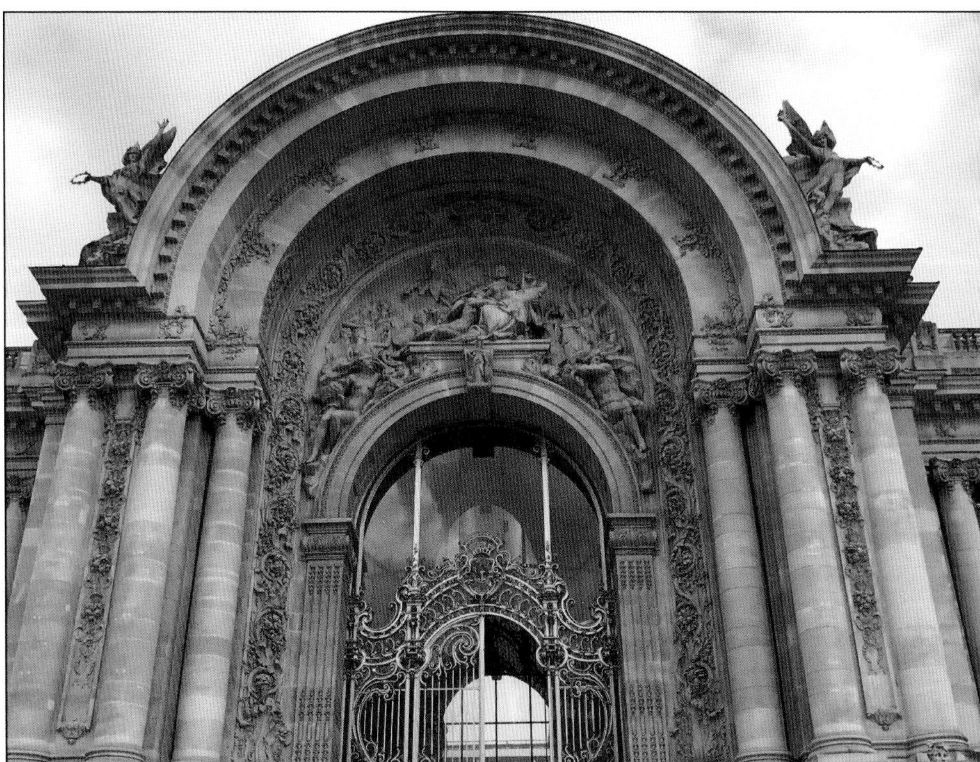

A closer view of the Petit Palais reveals an elaborate entry portal with heavenly sculptures simulating the majesty of a Gothic cathedral, albeit without religious modesty. Alexander Cassatt probably climbed these same steps when he traveled to Paris in 1900 for the opening of the Gare d'Orsay, a railway station built for the exposition. The architectural style undoubtedly impressed him and influenced the design of Pennsylvania Station. (Photograph by Gregory Bilotto.)

The École des Beaux-Arts was the premier Parisian architectural school. Founded in 1648 by the prime minister Cardinal Jules Mazarin (1602–1661) under King Louis XIV (1638–1715), its influence remained extensive. During the 19th and early 20th centuries, nearly every American architect was educated at the academy or was trained by a graduate. This image shows the Beaux-Arts façade and forecourt of the academy today. (Photograph by Gregory Bilotto.)

Legendary architect and playboy Stanford White, the genius behind numerous architectural achievements, including many design elements of the future Pennsylvania Station, is seen in this 1900 portrait. He was trained by one of the most successful architects in American history, Henry Hobson Richardson (1838–1886), a graduate of the École des Beaux Arts. (Courtesy of the Miscellaneous Photo Collection, LOC Prints and Photographs Division.)

Stanford White partnered with two other Beaux-Arts architects to establish the firm McKim, Mead, and White in 1879; the latter two had been in partnership since 1872. This portrait shows William Rutherford Mead (1846–1928), an architect with a love for Italy who was also a cousin of 19th US Pres. Rutherford Hayes (1822–1893). He was credited with introducing the Renaissance Revival style in America and subsequently was knighted in 1902 by King Vittorio Emanuele III (1869–1947) of Italy. (Courtesy of the Member Photograph Albums Collection in the Century Association Archives.)

Charles McKim is pictured in this portrait taken between 1890 and 1909 by the photographer Frances Benjamin Johnston (1864–1952). Similar to his architectural mentor, Henry Hobson Richardson, he graduated from Harvard University and the prestigious École des Beaux Arts. Recent research has exposed the lascivious habits of McKim, Mead, and White through their participation in parties and other activities of upper-class society in the Gilded Age. (Courtesy of the Frances Benjamin Johnston Collection, LOC Prints and Photographs Division.)

European architectural styles influenced many notable buildings designed by Stanford White and his colleagues. A European dominance reverberated in Pennsylvania Station, and amazingly, some aspects from these earlier projects were integrated as well. This image of the Lovely Lane United Methodist Church (1884) in Baltimore shows a campanile modeled after a 12th century abbey in Pomposa, Italy. Here Stanford White has applied the Romanesque Revival style. (Photograph by Gregory Bilotto.)

A design for the Metropolitan Club at 1 East Sixtieth Street on Fifth Avenue by McKim, Mead, and White brought elements from Renaissance Revival style architecture, including fenestration defined by corbels, eaves-cornices, and the palazzo-sized floors together with components from the Beaux-Arts style. The columned arcade was applied to a similar design at Pennsylvania Station. The club, founded by John Pierpont Morgan (1837–1913) and Cornelius Vanderbilt, was constructed between 1891 and 1894. (Photograph by Gregory Bilotto.)

The Bowery Savings Bank (1895) by McKim, Mead, and White on Bowery and Grand Street was perhaps the most impressive example of the Beaux-Arts style in New York. Elements from its classical ornamentation can be traced directly to Pennsylvania Station, including the barrel-vaulted and coffered grand entry, Corinthian order columns, triangular pediments, and elaborate sculptures by Frederick MacMonnies (1863–1937). This photograph showing the elevated Third Avenue Line was taken in 1905. (Courtesy of the Detroit Publishing Company Collection, LOC Prints and Photographs Division.)

A second clubhouse designed by the firm, but with strong influence from Charles McKim, between 1897 and 1900 and located at 1 West Fifty-Fourth Street on Fifth Avenue embraced the Renaissance Revival style together with the Beaux-Arts style. The University Club boasts eaves-cornices and large arched windows, and its massive palazzo design offers a rusticated quality. Many of these features, especially its imposing monumentality, would be present at Pennsylvania Station. (Photograph by Gregory Bilotto.)

Stanford White, inspired by the 16th century Palazzo Grimani di San Luca on the Venetian Grand Canal, completed the Tiffany and Company Building between 1903 and 1906. The project, commissioned by the luxury designer to be its offices at 409 Fifth Avenue and East Thirty-Seventh Street, was realized before the construction of Pennsylvania Station. Details from the Renaissance Revival and Beaux-Arts styles are evident, which demonstrate a persistent affinity for classical European designs. (Photograph by Gregory Bilotto.)

Nearby, an example was constructed from 1906 to 1914 following the Beaux-Arts style popularized by McKim, Mead, and White. The Benjamin Altman and Company Building, a trendy department store, built in tandem with Pennsylvania Station by the rival firm Trowbridge and Livingston on Fifth Avenue and East Thirty-Fourth Street, demonstrated that palazzo influences remained pervasive. (Photograph by Gregory Bilotto.)

Similar to the Bowery Savings Bank, the Cable Building, erected between 1892 and 1894 at 621 Broadway and Houston Street, has retained many elements later utilized in Pennsylvania Station. These consisted of acanthus corbels, large arched windows, and numerous examples of intricate French ornamentation. Unlike the luxury department store needed by Benjamin Altman and Company, the Broadway and Seventh Avenue Railroad Company required a structure that could primarily mask its power infrastructure. (Photograph by Gregory Bilotto.)

An outstanding feature of the Beaux-Arts Cable Building, and even more critical since it survives today, was the extravagant entry portal sculpture. The company, undoubtedly flouting wealth generated from its cabled streetcars, installed a pair of 11-foot-high classically dressed women: *Liberty* with a torch (left), and *Justice* with a sword (later altered to another torch), which once framed a clock. The women, produced by the sculptor John Massey Rhind (1860–1936), would form a nearly identical arrangement at Pennsylvania Station. (Photograph by Gregory Bilotto.)

Another project undertaken by McKim, Mead, and White was the Madison Square Presbyterian Church, formerly located on Madison Avenue at East Twenty-Fourth Street. The Beaux-Arts church, constructed between 1904 and 1906 and shown in this 1906–1910 image, was a derivative version of the second-century Pantheon in Rome. Although razed in 1919, its classical porch and triangular pediment were seemingly transposed to the façade of Pennsylvania Station. In actuality, much of the building was incorporated into the Beaux-Arts Hartford Times Building (1920) in Hartford, Connecticut. (Courtesy of the Detroit Publishing Company Collection, LOC Prints and Photographs Division.)

The Municipal Building at Chambers and Centre Streets, erected between 1907 and 1916, nears completion in this 1912 image. Devised by McKim, Mead, and White, despite the death of Stanford White in 1906, the project reveals that the Beaux-Arts style with Renaissance Revival influences had enduring popularity. The junior architect William Mitchell Kendall (1856–1941) was responsible for finishing its design, which was premised on the 16th century Palazzo Farnese in Rome. (Courtesy of the Miscellaneous Photo Collection, LOC Prints and Photographs Division.)

Following the destruction of Pennsylvania Station, the Municipal Building remains today a rare example of the classical temple design perfected by McKim, Mead, and White. The Beaux-Arts skyscraper still retains original details, including sculptures by Adolph Weinman (1870–1952)—*Civic Duty*, *Guidance*, and *Progress*—in the interstitial spaces between the Corinthian order columns and spandrels of the façade. (Photograph by Gregory Bilotto.)

A crowning achievement of Stanford White was his realization of Madison Square Garden (1890) at Madison Avenue and Twenty-Sixth Street. He was so fond of the entertainment complex that his apartment was located within its premises. Augustus Saint-Gaudens (1848–1907), a participant in the licentious activities, modeled the statue *Diana*, Roman goddess of the hunt, to crown its tower. This image was taken between 1900 and 1910 before the building was razed in 1926. (Courtesy of the Detroit Publishing Company Collection, LOC Prints and Photographs Division.)

The actress Evelyn Nesbit (1884–1967), wife of wealthy industrialist Harry Kendall Thaw (1871–1947), proved too irresistible for Stanford White. His affair with her culminated in an ironic tragedy that can be likened to the poolside murder of Jay Gatsby in F. Scott Fitzgerald's (1896–1940) *The Great Gatsby*. For this image, Stanford White had taken his mistress to the photography studio of Gertrude Käsebier (1852–1934) in 1900. (Courtesy of the Miscellaneous Photo Collection, LOC Prints and Photographs Division.)

The infamous Harry Kendall Thaw (seated) posed for this extradition photograph with Canadian law enforcement in December 1914. He had shot Stanford White to death on June 25, 1906, in the rooftop restaurant of Madison Square Garden before a crowd of hundreds. In a script from a Hollywood movie, he was tried, convicted, incarcerated, escaped, captured, and extradited as a fugitive from Canada. (Courtesy of the Miscellaneous Photo Collection, LOC Prints and Photographs Division.)

Delphin M. Delmas (1844–1928), the powerful California attorney for the drug-addicted Harvard dropout Harry Kendall Thaw, sat for this portrait in 1900. Even though he was successful in sparing his client a death sentence for premeditated murder, the verdict was undetermined, and a second trial soon followed. (Courtesy of the Miscellaneous Photo Collection, LOC Prints and Photographs Division.)

The "trial of the century" upended Gilded Age society, and crowds waited for the salacious details. Here, the public queues outside the courthouse probably during the first proceedings in January 1907. During his second trial, Harry Kendall Thaw was declared insane and incarcerated at Matteawan State Hospital for the Criminally Insane in Matteawan (Beacon), New York. In 1913, he escaped to Canada, presumably through the influence of his mother's wealth. (Courtesy of the Bain News Service Collection, LOC Prints and Photographs Division.)

Alexander Cassatt, an engineer and the seventh president of the Pennsylvania Railroad, posed for this portrait between 1890 and 1900. He was the patriarch of a spectacularly wealthy Philadelphia family, and his sister was the famous impressionist Mary Cassatt (1844–1926). He perpetuated a long-term Gilded Age rivalry with the competing railway after expanding direct rail access into New York. His vision to construct a superior train station culminated in Pennsylvania Station. (Courtesy of the Bain News Service Collection, LOC Prints and Photographs Division.)

An artist rendering of Pennsylvania Station produced during the early 1900s presents the vision imagined by Alexander Cassatt and Charles McKim. The Beaux-Arts structure followed an idealized version of the classical temple made famous in architecture during the Gilded Age. The style was intended to convey permanence, suggesting that these buildings had been built during antiquity. (Author's collection.)

This artist rendering from 1895 depicts the classically symmetrical Gare d'Orsay in Paris, which was constructed for the 1900 Universal Exhibition. The Beaux-Arts station, serving passengers on the Paris-Orléans Railway, represented the latest in French engineering and design. Alexander Cassatt traveled to Paris specifically to see the station during its grand opening. (Courtesy of the Miscellaneous Photo Collection, LOC Prints and Photographs Division.)

Designed by three graduates from the École des Beaux Arts, Victor Laloux (1850–1937), Lucien Magne (1849–1916), and Émile Bénard (1844–1929), the station was adorned with incredible Beaux-Arts details. These consisted of dentilled cornices, elaborate corbels, arched portals, triumphal garlands with fig leaves, heraldic crests, and sculptures, among others. Alexander Cassatt was impressed with the design, and the future Pennsylvania Station would incorporate many of these elements. (Photograph by Gregory Bilotto.)

The main entrance to Gare d'Orsay, although converted into Musée d'Orsay in 1986, features an enormous clock with a lion below. The lion, one had been placed above each entry, contains a caduceus with wings symbolizing Mercury. The Roman god was the guardian of transport and speed, meaning each lion "roared" a message of swift transportation. These classical symbols were typical of the Beaux-Arts style. A contemporary example can be found on the 1916 railway station in Bronxville, New York. (Photograph by Gregory Bilotto.)

The train shed, constructed from a cast-iron and glass superstructure, truly reflected the elegance and grandeur of the Beaux-Arts style because the interstitial spaces were filled with decorative coffering and rosettes. The electrified trains were hidden below grade, and elevators moved passengers and goods between platforms. At the opening, one critic remarked somewhat ironically that it resembled an art gallery more than a railway station. (Photograph by Gregory Bilotto.)

A pair of monumental gilt clocks with intricate ornamentation, including scrolls, triumphal garlands, and other foliate decoration, continue to keep time in the former train shed. It seemed that Alexander Cassatt was not the only interested party in Gare d'Orsay, since a graduate from the École des Beaux Arts—Whitney Warren (1864–1943), from the firm Warren and Wetmore—also incorporated many of these details into Grand Central Terminal. (Photograph by Gregory Bilotto.)

A closer view of the ornate decoration within the train shed reveals numerous references to classical antiquity and especially public buildings patronized by Roman emperors. These consisted of coffering with rosettes, garlands and heraldic imagery, and foliate decoration. For Beaux-Arts architects, the close association with Roman art and architecture was imperative because, in their minds, contemporary architecture was a noble undertaking. (Photograph by Gregory Bilotto.)

Between the massive arched windows and behind the gilt clocks at either end of the train shed, interior passages were added on multiple levels permitting movement across the concourse. This design was integrated into Grand Central Terminal both for natural lighting and ease of movement, which further proves the interest taken by the firm Warren and Wetmore. (Photograph by Gregory Bilotto.)

The tragic crash in the Montparnasse Railway Station was preserved in this iconic image, probably taken by Albert Brichaut (1864–?), on October 22, 1895. The steam-powered Granville-Paris Express failed to stop, crossed the platform, and crashed through the façade to the street below. A newsagent was killed, and passengers suffered minor injuries. Human negligence was the cause, and the crew was censured, but the shock of the tragedy was further justification for placement of the tracks below grade in Pennsylvania Station. (Courtesy of Wikimedia Commons.)

The Roman emperor Caracalla (188–217) ordered his namesake baths constructed during the third century in Rome. The massive complex contained a columned tepidarium sheathed in travertine marble and vaulted ceilings finished with large coffering. Both Alexander Cassatt and Charles McKim admired this architectural feat and, after their visit, radically altered the design of Pennsylvania Station. (Photograph by Gregory Bilotto.)

A closer view of the complex reveals the massive scale of the brick piers. This monumentality was reflected in the station, and especially the general waiting room, making it the fourth-largest structure in the world. After its opening, passengers imagined they had stepped into ancient Rome. It should not be surprising that a Roman imperial building was selected as the model for the station since it conveyed a sense of nobility and splendor, ideals inherent to the Beaux-Arts style. (Photograph by Gregory Bilotto.)

The groundwork for the future Pennsylvania Station began after the purchase and demolition of nearly 500 properties, leading to the displacement of 5,000–6,000 mostly disadvantaged residents. Looking north toward West Thirty-Third Street in this 1904 image, workers excavate the site of the future General Post Office Building between Eighth and Ninth Avenues. (Courtesy of the Photographs Archive Center, National Museum of American History of the Smithsonian Institution.)

This portrait of the Cooper-Union trained civil engineer John F. O'Rourke (1858–1934), president of the O'Rourke Engineering Construction Company, was taken on September 10, 1910. The 6,575-foot rail tunneling contracts connecting New York and New Jersey for the new Pennsylvania Station were awarded to his firm. He also received the excavation contract for Grand Central Terminal on May 2, 1904. (Courtesy of the Bain News Service Collection, LOC Prints and Photographs Division.)

The Keystone View Company produced this stereoscopic view of the excavation process as an elevated Ninth Avenue Line train rumbles past between 1907 and 1908. An incredible undertaking, the project required workers to navigate a myriad of building foundations, gas, sewer, and water lines, and the elevated train service, which remained operational. (Courtesy of the Stereograph Cards Collection, LOC Prints and Photographs Division.)

In this stereoscopic view also taken by the Keystone View Company around 1907–1908, workers harness the power of pneumatic drilling to transform the site expeditiously. The steam-powered drills forced a chisel to repeatedly hammer and fracture the rock more rapidly. (Courtesy of the Stereograph Cards Collection, LOC Prints and Photographs Division.)

A view into the excavation site toward Thirty-Third Street and Seventh Avenue in 1904 reveals a gloomy atmosphere created by steam and soot along with the severe working conditions for those at the site. At center, a steam-powered locomotive pulls a train of coal, the energy source for the steam-powered construction equipment. (Courtesy of the Photographs Archive Center, National Museum of American History of the Smithsonian Institution.)

In this undated photograph likely from 1904–1905, the excavation continues as management and workers with slickers stand adjacent to a section of the cast-iron frame used in the tunnel. The well-dressed man at center right is probably John F. O'Rourke. (Courtesy of the Photographs Archive Center, National Museum of American History of the Smithsonian Institution.)

Deep into a shaft, arduous work has begun for tunnel excavation in this image from 1904–1905. On either side of the river, deep shafts were dug, allowing the twin tunnels, each with a single track, to stretch below the river bottom. A pit railway, often found in mining operations and shown in the background, was employed to more easily facilitate the removal of rock and sludge. (Courtesy of the Photographs Archive Center, National Museum of American History of the Smithsonian Institution.)

Tunneling below the Hudson River was miserable and dangerous. Workers endured steam, smoke, and soot, along with intense physical activity. In this image from 1904–1905, and the next several, none of the workers appear to be aged above 30. The danger of a tunnel collapse or flood was another daily reality, as evidenced in October 1904, when water pierced the New York tunnel, triggering flooding. (Courtesy of the Photographs Archive Center, National Museum of American History of the Smithsonian Institution.)

The tunneling process required specialized equipment. Here, workers have paused from operations in an image from 1905–1906 with a tunneling shield. The machine, initially designed by Sir Marc Isambard Brunel (1769–1849) for a Thames River tunnel in London during the mid-1800s, was improved throughout the 19th century. (Courtesy of the Photographs Archive Center, National Museum of American History of the Smithsonian Institution.)

Charles Jacobs (1850–1919), an engineer with tunneling experience in the East River, was assigned to lead the Pennsylvania Railroad project and designed shields with a 23-foot diameter and 17-foot length. These shields, including the one in this 1906 image, utilized multiple hydraulic jacks to advance along the cast-iron framework. The rock was blasted, and then sludge passed through the shields, while waste would be carted along the pit railway. (Courtesy of the Photographs Archive Center, National Museum of American History of the Smithsonian Institution.)

The tunnels were dug 95 feet from the highest point of the Hudson River and were 25 feet below the river bottom. This avoided disturbances from periodic dredging, sunken vessels, passing ships, and existing bridge pylons. The process can be seen in this 1906 image. Although a pair of tunnels crossed the Hudson River from Bergen Hill, New Jersey, four more crossed the East River linking the Pennsylvania Railroad to the newly acquired Long Island Railroad. (Courtesy of the Photographs Archive Center, National Museum of American History of the Smithsonian Institution.)

In 1907, workers splashed with sludge operate a shield that applies pneumatic pressure to continue tunneling. Caulking and cement sealed the cast-iron superstructure, essentially creating a waterproof bond. Another safety consideration unfortunately omitted was the installation of concrete benches along the tunnels to guide trains during a derailment. (Courtesy of the Photographs Archive Center, National Museum of American History of the Smithsonian Institution.)

Surveyors collect measurements within the tunnel, ensuring that the grade is maintained, in this 1905–1906 image. Often during tunneling, especially midway through the Hudson River, sludge forced the shield to rise and thus altered the grade. As a result, the shields were not applied flush with the sediment but were angled downward. (Courtesy of the Photographs Archive Center, National Museum of American History of the Smithsonian Institution.)

An ironworker with a hammer pauses from waterproofing the cast-iron framing around 1906–1907. Tunnel sealing involved the hammering of caulk between cast-iron seams, making it ready for the concrete seal. The cast-iron superstructure, a novelty in tunnel building, enormously strengthened the tunnels. (Courtesy of the Photographs Archive Center, National Museum of American History of the Smithsonian Institution.)

Even though tunneling nears completion in this 1907 image, a final transport connection linking the Pennsylvania Railroad with a pathway to New England was not realized until 1916. The Hell Gate Bridge, a through-arch type, meaning the roadway crossed through the arch, was erected by the American Bridge Company. The Beaux-Arts bridge, made from steel and supported by massive stone piers, spanned the East River. (Courtesy of the Photographs Archive Center, National Museum of American History of the Smithsonian Institution.)

The June 1909 completion was celebrated by driving an open Lozier automobile through the tunnel, the first motor vehicle under the Hudson River, with passengers Charles Jacobs, John F. O'Rourke, and railroad vice president Samuel Rea (1855–1929), among others. The tunnel project was an incredible engineering achievement, and the shield machinery, operated by workers in this 1907 image, was perhaps even more of an achievement. Consequently, it was displayed at the 1904 Louisiana Purchase Exposition in Saint Louis. (Courtesy of the Photographs Archive Center, National Museum of American History of the Smithsonian Institution.)

This photograph, taken between 1904 and 1909, and the next two, offer an incredible glimpse into healthcare for the workers known colloquially as "sandhogs" due to their subterranean work. The immigrants, mostly from Eastern Europe, Ireland, and Italy, would fraternize in "sand-houses" before undertaking each day's dangerous work. Here, a physician conducts an examination in the offices of the O'Rourke Engineering Construction Company. (Courtesy of the Photographs Archive Center, National Museum of American History of the Smithsonian Institution.)

The doctor provides treatment for another worker in this image from the same series. The physical toll for workers was significant since tunneling operations ran 24 hours. The work was split into three eight-hour shifts, with each shield requiring 24 workers. At this rate, 18 feet were completed per day. The twin Hudson River tunnels necessitated the excavation of 190,000 cubic yards of earth, while 67,000 tons of iron and steel and 57,000 cubic yards of concrete were applied. (Courtesy of the Photographs Archive Center, National Museum of American History of the Smithsonian Institution.)

In the last photograph from the series, the same physician writes at his desk while a slickered worker emerges, the door still ajar, and a spittoon at his feet. Tunneling was incredibly dangerous, and it is thought that one worker died for every foot of tunnel in all the New York projects. After a spate of deaths in 1906, Progressive Era laws were passed to improve working conditions and safety. (Courtesy of the Photographs Archive Center, National Museum of American History of the Smithsonian Institution.)

Surface excavation continued simultaneously with the subterranean work. In this 1906 image, massive rocks have been sheared from Thirty-Third Street as a crowd of onlookers above watch from Eighth Avenue. Nearly all the stone extracted from the site and during the tunneling was crushed and used in concrete mixing or for railway track ballast. (Courtesy of the Photographs Archive Center, National Museum of American History of the Smithsonian Institution.)

Looking east from Ninth Avenue, the project has advanced in this August 1907 image. The construction equipment displays the name "George A. Fuller Company," the general contractor for Pennsylvania Station. George A. Fuller (1851–1900) founded his namesake company in 1882 and specialized in all aspects of construction except architectural designs. His general contracting model remains prevalent today. (Courtesy of the Avery Classics Collection, Avery Architectural and Fine Arts Library of Columbia University.)

A crowd of gawkers view the progress in April 1907. The excavation decimated the Tenderloin neighborhood of Hell's Kitchen, an area predominantly comprised of tenements and brothels. The New Yorkers who resided here were poor and unable to assert their rights. (Courtesy of the Photographs Archive Center, National Museum of American History of the Smithsonian Institution.)

Several accomplished artists, mostly from the Ashcan School, were compelled to capture images of daily work at the site. The artistic movement, popular during the late 19th and early 20th centuries, focused on the plight of the common worker. George Bellows (1882–1925), an original member, painted *Pennsylvania Excavation* in 1907 depicting two workers at lower right. Despite the lack of recognition, the workers were the real force leading the project to completion. (Courtesy of Smith College Museum of Art).

Another painting by George Bellows, *Pennsylvania Station Excavation*, from 1907, presents similar imagery. Here, the artist has attempted to dispel the glamor of the Gilded Age project and instead focuses on rising plumes of smoke and steam, while workers traverse a bleak, snow-filled pit. His emphasis on the despair of the worker evokes many questions about who would actually benefit from the new station. (Courtesy of the Brooklyn Museum of Art.)

In 1909, George Bellows completed *Blue Morning*, his third in a four-part series on Pennsylvania Station. It reveals the impressive Beaux-Arts station rising in the background, but more importantly, the focus remains on difficulties experienced by the workers. The fourth painting, *Excavation at Night*, from 1908, is today in the Crystal Bridges Museum of American Art. (Courtesy of the National Gallery of Art).

Ernest Lawson (1873–1939), another member of the Ashcan movement, also produced paintings of urban New York. In his 1906 work *Excavation Penn Station*, he highlighted the activities of workers at the site. A steam-powered locomotive chugs, cranes lift material, and the workers break apart large quantities of rock. (Courtesy of Wikimedia Commons.)

In November 1907, construction continues at the corner of Seventh Avenue and Thirty-First Street, while the retaining wall and steel viaduct for Seventh Avenue has been completed. At right is a rare view of the roadway construction process, as the riveted steel viaduct and brickwork for Thirty-First Street advance. (Courtesy of the Avery Classics Collection, Avery Architectural and Fine Arts Library of Columbia University.)

Reminiscent of the painting by George Bellows, snow has covered the excavation site in this December 1907 photograph. Looking toward the retaining wall for Seventh Avenue, the steel framing of the station continues, and the viaduct at Thirty-First Street has been finished. The subterranean spaces below the viaducts would be incorporated into the station. (Courtesy of the Avery Classics Collection, Avery Architectural and Fine Arts Library of Columbia University.)

By January 1908, the steel fabrication work had progressed. This image exposes a razed neighborhood where some of the poorest New Yorkers had been cast aside. The Pennsylvania Railroad acquired most of the properties necessary, including entire tenements, and although landlords received compensation, the impoverished tenants did not. (Courtesy of the Avery Classics Collection, Avery Architectural and Fine Arts Library of Columbia University.)

There were a few exceptions when the Pennsylvania Railroad was obliged to provide adequate compensation, including the Church of Saint Michael. The Catholic church, constructed from Indiana limestone and consecrated in 1894 at Ninth Avenue between Thirty-First and Thirty-Second Streets, was deconstructed and relocated to 424 West Thirty-Fourth Street between Ninth and Tenth Avenues. Rebuilt in 1904, it cost $1 million and today remains a lasting by-product of the lost railway station. (Photograph by Gregory Bilotto.)

This 1908 image was taken from the massive pit of the future General Post Office Building, looking toward the Eighth Avenue viaduct with Thirty-Third Street on the left. As the station rises in the background, a temporary railway, assembled over what had been Thirty-Second Street, can be seen with a steam-powered locomotive, much like in the 1906 work of Ernest Lawson. (Courtesy of the Detroit Publishing Company Collection, LOC Prints and Photographs Division.)

In this image from June 1908, Macy's Herald Square towers in the distance. The 1901 department store, designed in the Renaissance Revival style by the firm De Lemos and Cordes, was a product of the George A. Fuller Company. Here, the steel superstructure of the station has advanced and would be completed within two years. (Courtesy of the Avery Classics Collection, Avery Architectural and Fine Arts Library of Columbia University.)

Looking toward the rear of Pennsylvania Station from the corner of Eighth Avenue and Thirty-First Street in September 1908, the steel frame construction has advanced. Horse-drawn wagons, still a necessary form of transport around the site, wait patiently for their next tasks. Advertisements for current shows have been pasted on barrels along Eighth Avenue. (Courtesy of the Avery Classics Collection, Avery Architectural and Fine Arts Library of Columbia University.)

A closer view from the same vantage in October 1908 reveals the intricate maze of steelwork construction, which would soon be shielded in glass and stone. Pennsylvania Station was avant-garde in many ways; from the general contracting model to the reinforced steel superstructure, the building represented the very latest in engineering and technology. (Courtesy of the Bain News Service Collection, LOC Prints and Photographs Division.)

A photographer on a Thirty-First Street rooftop looked toward the elevated Ninth Avenue Line to capture this image in October 1908. Here, a section of Thirty-Second Street was demolished, and a temporary railway trestle was constructed to remove excavation debris. It would soon give way to the new General Post Office Building in 1912. (Courtesy of the Bain News Service Collection, LOC Prints and Photographs Division.)

The grand entry emerges on Seventh Avenue, proudly displaying advertising from the George A. Fuller Company in another image from October 1908. An element of the façade ornamentation consisted of relief sculptures by Adolph Weinman, symbolizing travel and speed through the caduceus and the wings of Hermes, which were draped in Roman triumphal garlands. (Courtesy of the Bain News Service Collection, LOC Prints and Photographs Division.)

A second view of the entry façade on Seventh Avenue in October 1908 shows the grandeur and large scale of the station. The steel superstructure was sheathed in Milford pink granite, a prized luxury that undoubtedly displayed the wealth and power of the Pennsylvania Railroad. (Courtesy of the Avery Classics Collection, Avery Architectural and Fine Arts Library of Columbia University.)

The entry façade, with its Doric order columns and capitals made from Milford pink granite, is seen here in November 1908. The impressive stone, quarried exclusively in Milford, Massachusetts, has been exhausted, but it can be found today in several Gilded Age New York structures, including the General Post Office Building and the Beaux-Arts American Museum of Natural History (1874). (Courtesy of the Avery Classics Collection, Avery Architectural and Fine Arts Library of Columbia University.)

In January 1909, steam-powered rollers and horse-drawn wagons work feverishly to complete Seventh Avenue. The columned arcade occupied the entirety of the block, while an elaborate triangular pediment marked both exits. Upon entering the central portal, passengers passed through a sizable columned pavilion stretching 75 feet high and 102 feet wide. (Courtesy of the Avery Classics Collection, Avery Architectural and Fine Arts Library of Columbia University.)

In February 1909, progress was made on the Seventh Avenue roadway and the exceptional sculptural composition adorning the central portal by Adolph Weinman in Tennessee pink marble. A pair of women—*Day*, with open eyes and sunflowers, and *Night*, with closed eyes and a cape—flank a triumphal wreath with space for a clock. This arrangement was reproduced over the other three entrances. (Courtesy of the Avery Classics Collection, Avery Architectural and Fine Arts Library of Columbia University.)

As the Seventh Avenue façade neared completion in September 1909, the Beaux-Arts details became more visible. Aside from classical sculptures and relief panels, additional elements included the balustrades, dentilled cornicing, Doric order columns and pilasters, and the architraves. (Courtesy of the Avery Classics Collection, Avery Architectural and Fine Arts Library of Columbia University.)

The rear of the station, seen from Eighth Avenue and Thirty-Third Street in April 1909, reveals an enormous advance in construction. The avenue has been finished along with numerous administration offices delineated by symmetrical fenestration. Upon completion, the rear entry would lead passengers directly to the concourse. (Courtesy of the Avery Classics Collection, Avery Architectural and Fine Arts Library of Columbia University.)

This May 1909 image was taken from the roof of an adjacent building on Thirty-First Street, looking toward Eighth Avenue. It provides a complete view of the station with the New York Terminal Service Plant (1908) at right, its primary power source. (Courtesy of the Avery Classics Collection in the Avery Architectural and Fine Arts Library of Columbia University.)

Work continues on the massive general waiting room of Pennsylvania Station in April 1910. It measured 110 feet wide and 300 feet long. Supporting the 150-foot-high vaulted and coffered ceiling were eight enormous columns from the Corinthian order spanning 60 feet with a diameter of seven feet. The stepped entries leading from Thirty-First and Thirty-Third Streets were framed by an arcade of Ionic columns, while the walls were adorned with Ionic pilasters and dentilled cornices. (Courtesy of the Avery Classics Collection, Avery Architectural and Fine Arts Library of Columbia University.)

Preparing to open Pennsylvania Station, workers undertake the final stages during the summer of 1910. Tragically, so many central to the project had died before its completion, including George A. Fuller (1900), Stanford White (1906), Alexander Cassatt (1906), Charles McKim (1909), and many now anonymous immigrant workers. (Courtesy of the Avery Classics Collection, Avery Architectural and Fine Arts Library of Columbia University.)

This rear view of Pennsylvania Station from Eighth Avenue and Thirty-First Street in April 1910 reveals a nearly finished façade, since the clock still needs to be installed. The project required 27,000 tons of steel, 64,000 barrels of cement, 1 million cubic feet of stone and cinder to fireproof the concrete, and 17 million bricks. Across the avenue, work has begun on the General Post Office Building. (Courtesy of the Avery Classics Collection, Avery Architectural and Fine Arts Library of Columbia University.)

Perhaps the most recognizable image of Pennsylvania Station, taken from Thirty-Third Street and Seventh Avenue during winter 1910, this photograph shows the "temple of transportation" preparing for its opening. In one of the many ironies, the building, intended to resurrect Roman antiquity and last for centuries, would have a shockingly brief lifespan of just 53 years. (Courtesy of the Detroit Publishing Company Collection, LOC Prints and Photographs Division.)

At 10:17 a.m., Seventh Avenue and Thirty-Second Street were unusually quiet for this photograph during spring 1910 before the opening of Pennsylvania Station. The majestic sculptures and clock, inspired by the design for the Cable Building by Stanford White in 1894, flanked by six majestic eagles, a reference to Roman imperial power, exemplified the spirit of the Beaux-Arts style. (Courtesy of the Detroit Publishing Company Collection, LOC Prints and Photographs Division.)

Three

The Early Years and Gilded Age Competition

The announcement by the Pennsylvania Railroad of a new purpose-built transport center in Midtown Manhattan accessible via multiple tunnel and bridge connections prompted immediate action from the rival railway and the Vanderbilt family. Pennsylvania Station, the pride of the Pennsylvania Railroad, would facilitate direct access for passengers and freight into New York for the first time and thereby threaten the powerful Vanderbilt monopoly. Recognizing the long-term financial implications and the potential loss of Vanderbilt power and prestige, two architecture firms merged at the behest of William Kissam Vanderbilt. Warren and Wetmore, along with Reed and Stem, formed Associated Architects and quickly developed plans for Grand Central Terminal, an equally impressive Beaux-Arts structure intended to surpass Pennsylvania Station. These projects, typical of the Gilded Age, pressed prestigious architecture firms to design increasingly grander and more expensive buildings, which fueled antagonism among the wealthiest companies and families. For the latter, demonstrations of power were manifested through self-aggrandizement, including Cornelius Vanderbilt, William Kissam Vanderbilt, and Alexander Cassatt, that resulted in illuminated displays of their names or oversized bronze statues.

It was not considered unusual when a 12-foot-high bronze likeness of Cornelius Vanderbilt was erected above the entrance to the Hudson River Railroad freight depot in Saint John's Park. Designed by Albert de Groot (1810–1884) and sculpted by Ernst Plassmann (1823–1873) in 1869, the statue was set into a monumental frieze with imagery from his railway and shipping empire. The $500,000 display, more reminiscent of an ancient Roman imperial triumph or a Medici family tomb in Renaissance Florence, was ill-suited for an industrial depot, but Cornelius Vanderbilt wanted to broadcast his authority and power. The statue was reinstalled at Grand Central Terminal, undoubtedly to match its contemporary, the 10-foot-high bronze sculpture of Alexander Cassatt created by Adolph Weinman. The Pennsylvania Railroad president's likeness was prominently displayed in a classical niche that towered above the passengers. Such ostentatious and hubristic busts had not been witnessed on this scale since those commissioned by victorious Roman emperors, and the Classical Revival elements within their Beaux-Arts surroundings should not be overlooked. These powerful titans had reached into the past to appropriate Roman imagery and architecture, which they hoped would allow their authority and legitimacy to permeate through the thin gold veneer of the Gilded Age.

This view of Pennsylvania Station from Seventh Avenue and Thirty-Third Street with traffic police at center was taken in 1910. The station celebrated the New York–Long Island connection with great fanfare on September 8, 1910, and then with full service on November 27, 1910. Long Islanders celebrated "tunnel day" as the first train passed through suburban stations, while 100,000 people surged into the station during the November grand opening marveling at the new "Roman temple." (Courtesy of the Avery Classics Collection, Avery Architectural and Fine Arts Library of Columbia University.)

The play *Hanky Panky* advertised on Thirty-Third Street, at far right, indicates this photograph was taken between August and November 1912, its running time at the Broadway Theatre, which once stood at 1445 Broadway. A now fully operational Pennsylvania Station allowed passengers to enter tunnels in Bergen Hill, New Jersey, travel under the Hudson River, and arrive at Thirty-Fourth Street and Seventh Avenue. For Long Island, they continued under East River tunnels through Sunnyside Yard in Queens. After 1916, a connection from the station went to New England via Hell Gate Bridge. (Courtesy of the Detroit Publishing Company Collection, LOC Prints and Photographs Division.)

Spurred by the development of Pennsylvania Station, vacant land on Seventh Avenue between Thirty-Second and Thirty-Third Streets accommodated the Hotel Pennsylvania and Gimbel's department store in 1910. The latter, built in 1910 by Beaux-Arts architect Daniel Burnham (1846–1912) as its flagship, earned astronomical profits from railway traffic. The store, founded by Adam Gimbel (1817–1896) in 1887, was a significant competitor of Macy's Herald Square. By the 1960s, the area around Pennsylvania Station supported several lucrative department stores. (Courtesy of the Detroit Publishing Company Collection, LOC Prints and Photographs Division.)

Pennsylvania Station construction, initiated during summer 1906 and completed on August 1, 1910, when this photograph was taken, necessitated 27,000 tons of steel; 64,000 barrels of cement; 17 million bricks; 660,000 cubic feet of granite, marble, travertine, and artificial stone; and 563,000 square feet of granite, marble, travertine, cork, and maple for flooring. The total project cost $114 million, the equivalent of several billion dollars today. (Courtesy of the Detroit Publishing Company Collection, LOC Prints and Photographs Division.)

This view of the general waiting room taken before opening in 1910 reveals the influence from the classical world and recalls architectural details from many projects, including the Bowery Savings Bank and Metropolitan Club previously undertaken by McKim, Mead, and White. Further decoration in the main hall by renowned muralist Jules Guérin (1866–1946) consisted of six rectangular panels below the lunette windows depicting the routes of the Pennsylvania Railroad and Long Island Railroad. (Courtesy of the Avery Classics Collection, Avery Architectural and Fine Arts Library of Columbia University.)

The general waiting room, clad in travertine marble from a quarry near Tivoli, Italy, and also paved with marble, was equipped with baggage and parcel storage, public telephones, telegraph services, and ticketing windows. These can be seen adjacent to the columns in 1910. The baggage area connected to carriage drives for collection or delivery and to elevators that facilitated the movement of baggage wagons between platforms. (Courtesy of the Detroit Publishing Company Collection, LOC Prints and Photographs Division.)

Looking from the loggia, with the Alexander Cassatt statue at left in 1910, the concourse can be seen through the glass. The stairs at left and right led to the dining room and lunch counter, respectively, and the passage behind the photographer was the shopping arcade. During the day, the station was illuminated with several lunette windows and light wells; the former could vent hot air, while numerous globe-shaped lamps and sconces brightened each night. (Courtesy of the Detroit Publishing Company Collection, LOC Prints and Photographs Division.)

In a testament to the Gilded Age enmity between the rival railways, a 10-foot bronze statue of Alexander Cassatt sculpted by Adolph Weinman was set into the loggia at Pennsylvania Station, seemingly to remind passengers of the visionary behind its creation. Similarly, a 12-foot bronze statue of Cornelius Vanderbilt designed by Albert de Groot and sculpted by Ernst Plassmann had been placed at Grand Central Terminal, steps from the former Commodore Hotel. (Courtesy of the Miscellaneous Photo Collection, LOC Prints and Photographs Division.)

The station supported three floors of offices for railway administration, housing for 175 railway employees with toilet and bathing facilities, separate accommodation for the station master and his staff, locker rooms, a hospital, and police station. An assembly hall, billiard room, bowling alley, gymnasium, lecture rooms, and a library with a reading room were operated on the premises for employees by the Railroad YMCA. Additional amenities included a pair of private waiting rooms for funeral corteges. (Courtesy of the Avery Classics Collection, Avery Architectural and Fine Arts Library of Columbia University.)

Aside from sculptures and ornamentation, the oversized scale, demonstrated in this 1910 image, was extended to the general waiting rooms in both flagship railway stations. At Pennsylvania Station, the hall was built even more massive than its ancient Roman inspiration, the tepidarium in the Baths of Caracalla, while the celestial ceiling in the corresponding hall at Grand Central Terminal reached the heavens. (Courtesy of the Avery Classics Collection, Avery Architectural and Fine Arts Library of Columbia University.)

Criticism of Pennsylvania Station from contemporary architectural experts was premised on its grand classical design and modern reincarnation of a "Roman public building," which can be seen in this 1911 image. The French critic Augustin-Adolphe Rey (1864–1934), trained at the École des Beaux-Arts, had visited the site during construction in 1908 and was astonished to learn it would be a railway station. In his mind, it resembled a "Roman temple" and would have been more suited for a library. (Courtesy of Gregory Bilotto.)

McKim, Mead, and White envisioned that the carriage portals, on either end of the Seventh Avenue façade, would simulate entry through the Brandenburg Gate in Berlin. For the Doric façade on Seventh Avenue, the Tuscan colonnade by Giovanni Bernini (1598–1680), encapsulating the Basilica of Saint Peter in the Vatican, was the inspiration. Pennsylvania Station was modeled on examples of classical architecture, much like the monumental carriage drive parallel to Thirty-First Street in this 1911 image. (Courtesy of the Avery Classics Collection, Avery Architectural and Fine Arts Library of Columbia University.)

The loggia, an architectural necessity in ancient Roman buildings, was attached to the shopping arcade and provided access to the dining room and lunch counter. Looking toward the Thirty-First Street side in 1910, the loggia has been constructed with Ionic columns supporting an entablature with multiple levels of dentilled cornices. At right was the dining room; the brightly lit space at left was the shopping arcade. (Courtesy of the Detroit Publishing Company Collection, LOC Prints and Photographs Division.)

In this 1910 view of the shopping arcade looking through the loggia toward the general waiting room, with the dining room at left and the lunch counter at right, many of the shops remained vacant. The high and open ceilings allowed air to pass throughout the station and increased the impression of monumentality. The walls, decorated with Ionic order pilasters and dentilled cornices, were sheathed in travertine marble, while the floor was surfaced in another marble. (Courtesy of the Detroit Publishing Company Collection, LOC Prints and Photographs Division.)

This view through the crowded shopping arcade toward the pavilion and Seventh Avenue was captured in 1911. Passengers bustle in the busy arcade after 63,000 square feet of retail space had been occupied. Gimbel's had opened just outside only a year earlier, and several additional department stores would soon follow, offering further retail options. (Courtesy of the Miscellaneous Photo Collection, LOC Prints and Photographs Division.)

Included in the shopping arcade was this drugstore, which offered an assortment of nicely wrapped chocolates and a soda counter. According to a 1910 booklet printed by the Pennsylvania Railroad for its customers, the shops had been stocked carefully with items passengers would need during long-distance travel. This image and the next six were taken just before public opening or shortly after in September 1910. (Courtesy of the Detroit Publishing Company Collection, LOC Prints and Photographs Division.)

The main dining room, located off the retail arcade in the loggia, could comfortably seat 500 people. The food was prepared in an overhead kitchen and delivered via electric dumbwaiters. Diners were welcomed to an elegant room with the most exquisite French ornamentation, including a coffered ceiling, dentilled cornices, engaged columns, and pilasters in the Corinthian order, while lighting came from numerous arched windows by day and gilt chandeliers and globe-shaped lamps at night. (Courtesy of the Avery Classics Collection, Avery Architectural and Fine Arts Library of Columbia University.)

Much like the main dining room, the more informal lunch counter was ornately decorated with French details. Here, waiters patiently wait for the lunch crowd. The dining room and lunch counter undoubtedly offered a service comparable to the Oyster Bar in Grand Central Terminal, which opened in 1913. (Courtesy of the Avery Classics Collection, Avery Architectural and Fine Arts Library of Columbia University.)

Another amenity offered to passengers was a barbershop, located above the concourse, which can be seen through the large rear window. The shop had several chairs, hardwood seating with spittoons, shoe shine stands, and multiple globe-shaped gilt lamps. (Courtesy of the Avery Classics Collection, Avery Architectural and Fine Arts Library of Columbia University.)

A smaller ladies' waiting room or retiring room provided tranquility from the busy station for female passengers. More modest than its counterpart in Grand Central Terminal, it included wicker lounge chairs and writing desks with gilt lamps. (Courtesy of the Avery Classics Collection, Avery Architectural and Fine Arts Library of Columbia University.)

The larger ladies' waiting room, situated off the general waiting room, was adorned with Beaux-Arts details. These comprised a coffered ceiling with rosettes corresponding to the decorative scheme outlined by Adolph Weinman, dentilled cornicing, large arched windows that could be opened for ventilation, hardwood benches, and lighting from coffers, sconces, and chandeliers. (Courtesy of the Avery Classics Collection in the Avery Architectural and Fine Arts Library of Columbia University.)

A large men's waiting room, attached to the general waiting room, matched the ladies' room both in size and design. Together, the two rooms, sheathed in Milford pink granite, could seat 700 people and were a vast improvement over the accommodations offered by the Pennsylvania Railroad at Jersey City Station, but they still could not compete with the luxury offered at the future Grand Central Terminal. (Courtesy of the Avery Classics Collection, Avery Architectural and Fine Arts Library of Columbia University.)

The concourse, pictured in 1910, was built with an exposed latticed steel superstructure by Westinghouse, Church, Kerr, and Company. The engineering firm had designed the steel structures along with 18 sets of train gates and stairs leading from the concourse 28 feet below to the platforms. The company also was responsible for 11 island platforms that stretched 20–40 feet wide and 750–1,170 feet long. Even though the platforms were below grade, they were level with the carriages, an innovation permitting passengers to more easily access trains. (Courtesy of the Detroit Publishing Company Collection, LOC Prints and Photographs Division.)

Another view from 1910 reveals the complicated latticed steel-frame network of cross vaults and barrel arches. Instead of masonry, the interstitial spaces provided illumination through thousands of glazed panes. The use of architectural forms and the interplay with light, perfected in medieval French cathedrals centuries earlier, contributed to the unique nature of the concourse design. The flooring, manipulated further by lighting, included thousands of glass bricks allowing natural light to penetrate to the platforms below. (Courtesy of the Detroit Publishing Company Collection, LOC Prints and Photographs Division.)

The architects harnessed natural lighting in the station whenever possible through light wells, massive windows, and even in the glass brick flooring. As a result, an expansive and inviting atmosphere was created for passengers. In this 1910 image, light wells in steel and Guastavino tiled side vaults brighten the platforms below. (Courtesy of the Avery Classics Collection in the Avery Architectural and Fine Arts Library of Columbia University.)

The tiled vaults shown in this 1910 image were the latest technology developed by Rafael Guastavino (1842–1908). He founded the Guastavino Fireproof Construction Company to implement his tiling process, which employed multi-layered tiles with mortar and plaster for strength. These layers were sheathed in decorative glazed tiles that formed a fireproof barrier. Fires were a huge concern, especially since the Jersey City Station had burned in the late 19th century. (Courtesy of the Detroit Publishing Company Collection, LOC Prints and Photographs Division.)

Looking toward the latticed steel-framed superstructure of the concourse in 1910, light floods through windows and glass brick flooring to the lower concourse and platforms. The third rails allowed for electrification of the railway lines. Power for the new electrical infrastructure was generated at the New York Terminal Service Plant on Thirty-First Street between Seventh and Eighth Avenues. (Courtesy of the Detroit Publishing Company Collection, LOC Prints and Photographs Division.)

Guastavino tiling can be seen strengthening these masonry vaults in 1910. Rafael Guastavino had succeeded in combining structural integrity and fire safety with beauty, which placed his tilework in high demand. It was applied to many contemporary projects, including Grand Central Terminal and the Municipal Building. Another innovative business, the Otis Elevator Company, founded by Elisha Otis (1811–1861), invented a "moving stairway" or escalator, and the Pennsylvania Railroad ordered one for its flagship station. (Courtesy of the Detroit Publishing Company Collection, LOC Prints and Photographs Division.)

One drawback of Pennsylvania Station was its many stairs. Aside from accessibility issues for disabled passengers, they impeded overall movement within the station, particularly for those with baggage and small children. This error was rectified in Grand Central Terminal when rises were utilized throughout rather than multiple sets of stairs. This 1910 image by Samuel Gottscho (1875–1971) shows some of the many stairs passengers had to traverse. (Courtesy of the Gottscho-Schleisner Collection, LOC Prints and Photographs Division.)

Berenice Abbott (1898–1991) captured this view of the multilevel concourse between 1935 and 1938. Below the main concourse, an exit concourse was constructed that spanned 60 feet wide and 480 feet long to separate arriving and departing passengers. The exit stairs, at right, were accessible via the exit concourse, and the entry stairs, at left, were accessed from the main concourse and led directly to the platforms. (Courtesy of the Changing New York Collection, Miriam and Ira D. Wallach Art, Prints, and Photographs Division, NYPL.)

Berenice Abbott took this photograph of the concourse during the same period while working for the Works Progress Administration to document an ever-changing New York. A distinguished American photographer, she was keen to preserve natural and pure images without any staging or posing. The midday sun is about to pierce the glass canopies, and the station will come alive, as the clock reads after 11:00 a.m. (Courtesy of the Changing New York Collection, Miriam and Ira D. Wallach Art, Prints, and Photographs Division, NYPL.)

Although this image was taken in the early 1960s, it offers a closer view of the concourse and gives an idea of the total labor-hours and volume of materials needed to finish the project, which was staggering. In the entire station, the roofing totals amounted to 450,000 square feet of metal and tile, 80,000 square feet of glass installed by glaziers, and 83,000 square feet of light wells incorporated into the design. (Courtesy of the Historic American Buildings Survey, LOC Prints and Photographs Division.)

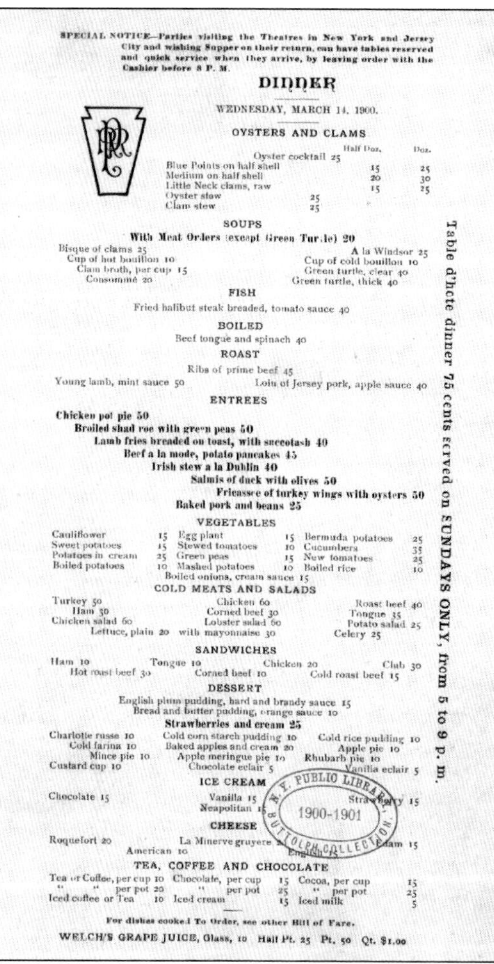

SPECIAL NOTICE—Parties visiting the Theatres in New York and Jersey City and wishing Supper on their return, can have tables reserved and quick service when they arrive, by leaving order with the Cashier before 8 P. M.

DINNER

WEDNESDAY, MARCH 14, 1900.

OYSTERS AND CLAMS

Oyster cocktail 25

	Half Doz.	Doz.
Blue Points on half shell	15	25
Medium on half shell	20	30
Little Neck clams, raw	15	25

Oyster stew 25
Clam stew 25

SOUPS

With Meat Orders (except Green Turtle) 20

Bisque of clams 25 — A la Windsor 25
Cup of hot bouillon 10 — Cup of cold bouillon 10
Clam broth, per cup 15 — Green turtle, clear 40
Consommé 20 — Green turtle, thick 40

FISH

Fried halibut steak breaded, tomato sauce 40

BOILED

Beef tongue and spinach 40

ROAST

Ribs of prime beef 45
Young lamb, mint sauce 50 — Loin of Jersey pork, apple sauce 40

ENTREES

Chicken pot pie 50
Broiled shad roe with green peas 50
Lamb fries breaded on toast, with succotash 40
Beef a la mode, potato pancakes 45
Irish stew a la Dublin 40
Salmis of duck with olives 50
Fricassee of turkey wings with oysters 50
Baked pork and beans 25

VEGETABLES

Cauliflower	15	Egg plant	15	Bermuda potatoes	25
Sweet potatoes	15	Stewed tomatoes	10	Cucumbers	35
Potatoes in cream	25	Green peas	15	New tomatoes	25
Boiled potatoes	10	Mashed potatoes	10	Boiled rice	10

Boiled onions, cream sauce 15

COLD MEATS AND SALADS

Turkey 50 — Chicken 60 — Roast beef 40
Ham 30 — Corned beef 30 — Tongue 35
Chicken salad 60 — Lobster salad 60 — Potato salad 25
Lettuce, plain 20 with mayonnaise 30 — Celery 25

SANDWICHES

Ham 10 — Tongue 10 — Chicken 20 — Club 30
Hot roast beef 30 — Corned beef 10 — Cold roast beef 15

DESSERT

English plum pudding, hard and brandy sauce 15
Bread and butter pudding, orange sauce 10
Strawberries and cream 25
Charlotte russe 10 — Cold corn starch pudding 10 — Cold rice pudding 10
Cold farina 10 — Baked apples and cream 20 — Apple pie 10
Mince pie 10 — Apple meringue pie 10 — Rhubarb pie 10
Custard cup 10 — Chocolate eclair 5 — Vanilla eclair 5

ICE CREAM

Chocolate 15 — Vanilla 15 — Strawberry 15
Neapolitan 15

CHEESE

Roquefort 20 — La Minerve gruyere [illegible] — Edam 15
American 10 — English 15

TEA, COFFEE AND CHOCOLATE

Tea or Coffee, per cup	10	Chocolate, per cup	15	Cocoa, per cup	15
" " per pot	20	" per pot	25	" per pot	25
Iced coffee or Tea	10	Iced cream	15	Iced milk	5

For dishes cooked To Order, see other Bill of Fare.

WELCH'S GRAPE JUICE, Glass, 10 Half Pt. 25 Pt. 50 Qt. $1.00

Table d'hote dinner 75 cents served on SUNDAYS ONLY, from 5 to 9 p. m.

Even though this March 1900 dinner menu predates Pennsylvania Station and had been produced for Jersey City Station, the selection and prices probably did not deviate much from the dining options in 1910. Interestingly, a quart of grape juice (all prices are in cents) cost more than any of the prepared meats, indicating that grapes remained a luxury import. Passengers traveling to shows in New York could pre-order meals for their return journey. (Courtesy of the Buttolph Menu Collection, Rare Book Division, NYPL.)

BREAKFAST
READY TO SERVE.

14 Mch. 1900

For Dishes Cooked To Order, See Bill Attached

Grapes	20
Grape fruit	25
Oranges	15
Bananas	10
Apples	10
Stewed prunes	10
Baked apples and cream	20
Pearl hominy and cream	20
Oatmeal and cream	20
Shredded wheat and cream	15
Broiled bluefish, drawn butter	40
Fish balls	25
Deerfoot Farm sausages	40
Broiled half chicken on toast	50
Pork chops	40
Broiled ham and eggs	45
Mutton chops	40
Broiled calf's liver and bacon	40
Small steak	45
Corned beef hash	25
Lyonnaise potatoes	10
Buckwheat cakes	15
Wheat cakes	15

This breakfast menu, probably offering similar choices to those found at the Pennsylvania Station lunch counter, was prepared for March 1900. Despite the breakfast and dinner menus offering extensive options, passengers could order à la carte as well. These menus represent a time when rail travel was highly lucrative and railway companies were competing for business. (Courtesy of the Buttolph Menu Collection, Rare Book Division, NYPL.)

The Beaux-Arts Grand Central Terminal, designed by Warren and Wetmore for the NYCHRR, opened in 1913. Modeled after medieval cathedrals in French towns where nothing could be taller, the terminal dominated the breadth of Park Avenue and could be seen for miles. Passengers arriving at the terminal in this 1914–1915 image are greeted by the soaring 48-foot *Glory of Commerce* by Jules-Félix Coutan (1848–1939) and a 13-foot-diameter stained-glass clock by Louis Comfort Tiffany (1848–1933). (Courtesy of the Detroit Publishing Company Collection, LOC Prints and Photographs Division.)

This image and the next six were taken in February 1913, after the terminal had been completed but before opening to the public. The images serve as a comparison to the rival Pennsylvania Station, which opened just three years earlier. Captured at night, the massive general waiting room awaits the first NYCHRR passengers, while incandescent lights brighten a constellation ceiling design by Paul-César Helleu (1859–1927), indicating that the terminal had reached the heavens. (Courtesy of the Detroit Publishing Company Collection, LOC Prints and Photographs Division.)

Inspired by stairs in the Palais Garnier (1875), the Second Empire and Beaux-Arts Parisian opera house, the interior of Grand Central Terminal invited passengers to travel in luxury. The intricate French ornamentation carved from Tennessee pink marble showcased the wealth and power of the railway, much like the Pennsylvania Railroad with its choice of Milford pink granite and travertine marble. The company rivalry was manifested even in the selection of stones. (Courtesy of the Detroit Publishing Company Collection, LOC Prints and Photographs Division.)

Taken at 12:23 a.m., a photographer looks toward the lower level as gilt chandeliers illuminate the rise from above. Levels of the terminal could be accessed via a series of rises or ramps, which planners had thoroughly tested and determined would be more efficient than stairs. This rise enabled passengers to pass between the main waiting room and the suburban concourse below. (Courtesy of the Detroit Publishing Company Collection, LOC Prints and Photographs Division.)

The lower-level suburban concourse allowed passengers to board trains for the New York and Connecticut suburbs. A significant part of the overall Grand Central Terminal project included the construction of several branch stations that would more easily facilitate rail travel into New York. In the image, French-inspired details can be observed on nearly every surface area, probably more than in Pennsylvania Station, since Whitney Warren had trained at the École des Beaux Arts for 10 years. (Courtesy of the Detroit Publishing Company Collection, LOC Prints and Photographs Division.)

The ladies' waiting room, furnished comfortably and imbued with mahogany paneling, offered lavatories and telephones. The French decoration extended to plaster-molded triumphal garlands, foliate motifs, and marble doorways, which differed from the more simplistic style in Pennsylvania Station. (Courtesy of the Detroit Publishing Company Collection, LOC Prints and Photographs Division.)

A seating area in the general waiting room, more reminiscent of a French palatial ballroom, allowed NYCHRR passengers a brief respite before departure. It was equipped with gilt chandeliers, hardwood benches, and tropical plants, while natural lighting illuminated the walls sheathed in Tennessee pink marble. Many of the intricately carved classical details were adorned with acorns and oak leaves. The mighty oak tree was a symbol of the Vanderbilt family. (Courtesy of the Detroit Publishing Company Collection, LOC Prints and Photographs Division.)

The incredibly lavish Oyster Bar, located between the main concourse and suburban level, was another amenity offered to passengers of the NYCHRR. The eatery had been furnished with imported luxuries including bentwood mahogany chairs produced by the famous Austrian furniture maker Jacob and Josef Kohn, oriental carpets, and tropical plants. Its vaulted ceilings were awash in decorative—and, more importantly, fireproof—Guastavino tiling. (Courtesy of the Detroit Publishing Company Collection, LOC Prints and Photographs Division.)

This bird's-eye view of Pennsylvania Station from 1916 shows the station and concourse, the adjacent General Post Office Building, and Gimbel's department store on Seventh Avenue between Thirty-Second and Thirty-Third Streets. The exposed tracks at the rear of the post office would be obscured by the West Annex (1939), which extended the building to Ninth Avenue. The neighborhood has been changed radically by many department stores, hotels, and offices. (Courtesy of the Popular Graphic Arts Collection, LOC Prints and Photographs Division.)

The Beaux-Arts General Post Office Building is shown after its completion in 1912. Designed by McKim, Mead, and White, two of them now were deceased, and William Mitchell Kendall saw it to completion. The structure was built entirely over railway tracks between Eighth and Ninth Avenues and Thirty-First and Thirty-Third Streets, thereby ensuring it would occupy the entire block. (Courtesy of the Detroit Publishing Company Collection, LOC Prints and Photographs Division.)

The building entry contained a 14-foot-high set of steps leading to a colonnade formed by a row of fluted columns with Corinthian capitals. Pavilions framed the steps and colonnade on Thirty-First and Thirty-Third Streets, but otherwise, it spanned 377 feet of Eighth Avenue uninterrupted. A photographer captured this image in 1914, revealing the retail gallery from within the Thirty-Third Street pavilion. (Courtesy of the Bain News Service Collection, LOC Prints and Photographs Division.)

The Beaux-Arts retail gallery retained unique elements of classical ornamentation. The geometrical ceiling, comprised of various lozenges and hexagons, was adorned with Roman foliate motifs and the emblems of 10 contemporary Western world powers. Alternating above each door and window were Corinthian triangular and lunette pediments. In this 1914 image, the gallery is illuminated by a fenestrated wall demarcated with Corinthian pilasters. At night, chandeliers lit the space. (Courtesy of the Bain News Service Collection, LOC Prints and Photographs Division.)

An elegant interior in the General Post Office Building, probably photographed in 1914, includes the latest in furnishings, including bookcases on either side of the doorway. These were produced by the Cincinnati-based Globe Wernicke Company, an office furniture manufacturer specializing in individually stacking cabinets. The novel shelves were constructed from hardwoods, notably mahogany, and were fitted with brass hardware. (Courtesy of the Bain News Service Collection, LOC Prints and Photographs Division.)

Aside from the retail gallery, the building contained mail sorting and delivery facilities. Here, postal workers pause from hand sorting for a photograph in 1914. In comparison to their peers, the sandhogs, these young men working at the new central postal building had attained a prized civil service job. (Courtesy of the Bain News Service Collection, LOC Prints and Photographs Division.)

In another image from 1914, a spittoon for chewing tobacco can be seen in the foreground while several young postal workers box mail. Below the post office, direct access to tracks enabled trains to shuffle mail via Pennsylvania Station across the country quickly. (Courtesy of the Bain News Service Collection, LOC Prints and Photographs Division.)

A final image from 1914 with many of the same postal workers highlights the pneumatic tube. Invented by William Murdoch (1754–1839) in 1799, these cylindrical tubes were powered by compressed air or vacuum pressure and allowed for the rapid transport of mail or other documents within a building. (Courtesy of the Bain News Service Collection, LOC Prints and Photographs Division.)

Four

The Later Years and Destruction

The decline of American railways, initially triggered by advances in automobiles and the interstate highway system and later through airplane travel, misguided urban planning, and mismanagement of railway expenses and resources, delivered a fatal blow to Pennsylvania Station. The failure of the Pennsylvania Railroad to prepare for future declines in rail travel and thereby profits left the company extremely vulnerable to insolvency. This situation was exacerbated by the absence of a constant revenue stream, namely office blocks, a hotel, or other onsite amenities that could have helped to bear the costs of maintaining the monumental station. In the end, the station was razed along with several vital public transport links, creating problems that remain today. Despite its unfortunate destruction, much of the public had been against its demolition, and some were proactive, which included picketing at the Seventh Avenue entrance and appealing to city government. Perhaps Ada Louise Huxtable (1921–2013), the renowned curator and architecture critic, summarized the case to preserve Pennsylvania Station best when she likened it to the colossal undertaking of the Parthenon, an achievement that would never again be possible.

The demise of the station was a shock to most New Yorkers, especially to the former first lady Jacqueline Kennedy Onassis (1929–1994), who spearheaded the campaign to preserve Grand Central Terminal from suffering a similar fate. Although the Vanderbilt terminal was saved, it came with a major caveat. The Pan American World Airways Building (Metropolitan Life Insurance Building today), designed by Walter Gropius (1883–1969), Pietro Belluschi (1899–1994), and Richard Roth (1904–1987) in the International style between 1959 and 1963, was attached to the rear of the terminal at 200 Park Avenue and Forty-Fifth Street. The new "supertall" building provided much-needed income, but initiated the sale of air rights in the Grand Central Terminal zone culminating with the unfortunate demolition of many buildings, including more recently the Liggett Building (1922) at 317 Madison Avenue and Forty-Second Street. The original Carrère and Hastings high-rise was lost to the massive supertall at One Vanderbilt Avenue. Construction of this new modern tower, designed by Kohn, Pedersen, and Fox Associates, began in 2017 and was completed in September 2020, when it became the fourth largest building in New York. Finally, the scandalous destruction of Pennsylvania Station and near loss of Grand Central Terminal directly resulted in the 1965 formation of the Landmarks Preservation Commission. This governmental board was tasked with listing, protecting, and approving any modifications to historic and notable buildings in New York City.

Joseph Delaney (1904–1991), a prominent black artist formerly employed by the Works Progress Administration, painted this 1943 wartime scene in Pennsylvania Station to record the actions of everyday Americans. *Penn Station at War* shows crowds of couples, the elderly, musicians, soldiers, tramps, and others continuing to travel through a station transformed by war. (Courtesy of the Smithsonian American Art Museum.)

In this image and those on the next 12 pages from August 1942, the wartime photographer Marjory Collins, working for the Office of War Information, preserved daily life in Pennsylvania Station while World War II continued. Much like her contemporary Joseph Delaney, she was fascinated by ordinary people, and in this photograph, she captured crowds on the busy concourse. (Courtesy of the US Farm Security Administration and Office of War Information Collection, LOC Prints and Photographs Division.)

Looking at the large crowd on the concourse, the importance of the railway station and growth in passenger volume seems evident. When this photograph was taken in 1942, Pennsylvania Station had experienced an enormous surge in travel, with a total of 42 million passengers. The volume increased over the next years, reaching its apex in 1945 with 109 million, or 350,000 on 900 trains each day. (Courtesy of the US Farm Security Administration and Office of War Information Collection, LOC Prints and Photographs Division.)

Seeing these passengers descend through the lower concourse to reach platform 13, the difficulties in accessing platforms, especially for passengers with baggage or those with disabilities, is abundantly clear. The many sets of stairs were an obstacle and a design flaw, particularly when compared to Grand Central Terminal with its series of rises and ramps. Although baggage lifts were available, most navigated stairs with baggage in hand. (Courtesy of the US Farm Security Administration and Office of War Information Collection, LOC Prints and Photographs Division.)

Pennsylvania Station, along with other key railway stations across the United States, was designated as critical for the movement of troops and potential evacuation of civilians. These stations were used for the sale of war bonds and to propagandize the war effort. Here, an oversized "victory" banner flanked by flags has been suspended in the concourse. (Courtesy of the US Farm Security Administration and Office of War Information Collection, LOC Prints and Photographs Division.)

In a scene reminiscent of the artwork produced by Joseph Delaney, a mass of people patiently wait to enter the lower concourse under patriotic banners and flags displayed above. Both Pennsylvania Station and Grand Central Terminal were vital for broadcasting positive messages to the traveling public, which was emphasized further when artists from the Works Progress Administration installed massive photographic murals in each general waiting room. (Courtesy of the US Farm Security Administration and Office of War Information Collection, LOC Prints and Photographs Division.)

These service personnel waiting for departures on the concourse would contribute to the ever-increasing passenger volume in Pennsylvania Station throughout the war. Although ridership peaked in 1945 during the mass demobilization after Allied victories in the European and Pacific theaters, numbers immediately declined thereafter. (Courtesy of the US Farm Security Administration and Office of War Information Collection, LOC Prints and Photographs Division.)

An information center was erected on the concourse to assist military personnel transiting through the station, which could rise exponentially when scores of draftees arrived. Interestingly, one background sign calls for civilians to "loan" binoculars to the US Navy for military reasons, likely to help identify enemy vessels and aircraft at sea. (Courtesy of the US Farm Security Administration and Office of War Information Collection, LOC Prints and Photographs Division.)

This view of the information desk in the general waiting room would soon be transformed by photo murals propagandizing the war. The 40-foot-high murals each highlighted a conductor, engineer, and porter, as well as a drafted marine, sailor, and soldier who cumulatively represented the contribution of the Pennsylvania Railroad to the war effort. A separate pair of banners honored drafted railway employees killed during the war. (Courtesy of the US Farm Security Administration and Office of War Information Collection, LOC Prints and Photographs Division.)

The United Service Organizations (USO) provided this sign announcing amenities for service members on the concourse. Founded in 1941 by Pres. Franklin Roosevelt (1882–1945) and Mary Ingram (1887–1981), the USO was an amalgamation of six charities that offered live entertainment and recreation for active-duty military personnel serving overseas. (Courtesy of the US Farm Security Administration and Office of War Information Collection, LOC Prints and Photographs Division.)

Service members wait with civilian passengers for departures to the West Coast. Military personnel departing Pennsylvania Station were destined for the Pacific, while those arriving were transferred to troopships headed to the European theater. The ocean liners *Queen Elizabeth* and *Queen Mary*, among others, were appropriated to transport soldiers and sailed predominantly from New York to ports in Europe. (Courtesy of the US Farm Security Administration and Office of War Information Collection, LOC Prints and Photographs Division.)

Three black service members wait for departures. Although segregation was not legal in the northern states, it was codified in the US armed forces. The practice was officially repealed following World War II by Pres. Harry Truman (1884–1972) on July 26, 1948, but unfortunately, the law was not implemented fully until 1960. (Courtesy of the US Farm Security Administration and Office of War Information Collection, LOC Prints and Photographs Division.)

This is a view of the Union News Company kiosk on the concourse, which provided troops with last-minute conveniences. Aside from reporting on current events, the company operated these popular newsstands at all Pennsylvania Railroad stations. The company produced many images of everyday American life for its newspapers, some of which can be seen in this book. (Courtesy of the US Farm Security Administration and Office of War Information Collection, LOC Prints and Photographs Division.)

At 9:40 a.m., passengers and service members gather in the concourse for departures. These scenes soon would be viewed from a different perspective because a new glass-enclosed control tower was installed in 1946. The novel glass office was built for the stationmaster and allowed railway staff better observation of daily operations on the concourse. (Courtesy of the US Farm Security Administration and Office of War Information Collection, LOC Prints and Photographs Division.)

The station received a new reservation system known as the "Wassell Unit" during the 1940s. The invention consisted of nine revolving drums with holes for 44,000 colored pegs. Each hole represented a seat on a train, and the colored pegs indicated its status: reserved, occupied, or vacant. This system allowed the railway to track seating 90 days before departures. (Courtesy of the US Farm Security Administration and Office of War Information Collection, LOC Prints and Photographs Division.)

Before the war began, its imminent threat had elicited a careful preparatory response from the federal government and especially Pres. Franklin Roosevelt. As a result, major railways across the country were instructed to prepare plans to ensure uninterrupted operation of their lines and transport hubs. (Courtesy of the US Farm Security Administration and Office of War Information Collection, LOC Prints and Photographs Division.)

After the US entered the war, the Office of Defense Transportation was created to guarantee the movement of troops and supplies across the country via civilian railways. The first director appointed by the president was experienced railway workers' advocate Joseph Eastman (1882–1944). (Courtesy of the US Farm Security Administration and Office of War Information Collection, LOC Prints and Photographs Division.)

To facilitate rapid movement of troops during the war, the Pennsylvania Railroad appropriated 125 freight locomotives and refurbished thousands of disused freight cars at an astonishing cost, undoubtedly billed to the federal government. These wartime expenditures were the impetus for lifting the American economy out of the Great Depression. (Courtesy of the US Farm Security Administration and Office of War Information Collection, LOC Prints and Photographs Division.)

The transport of service personnel held priority over civilian travel, leading to massive overcrowding on "normal" trains. These services were limited, and most passengers stood in aisles. Additionally, luxury cars had been requisitioned, much like the ocean liners, and were converted into hospitals or troop transports. (Courtesy of the US Farm Security Administration and Office of War Information Collection, LOC Prints and Photographs Division.)

Service members arriving at Pennsylvania Station, like these three sailors emerging from the lower concourse, were greeted with assistance from the American Red Cross. Although much support was provided by the USO, the Red Cross provided food and comfort to many, especially through its Red Cross Ship Service, which was extended into Pennsylvania Station. (Courtesy of the US Farm Security Administration and Office of War Information Collection, LOC Prints and Photographs Division.)

Looking into the general waiting room from the escalators, the "victory" banners in the concourse can be observed through the glass partition. This crowded space would support the war effort further when Metro-Goldwyn-Mayer filmed *The Clock* starring Judy Garland (1922–1969) and Robert Walker (1918–1951). Released in 1945, it was filmed partially at these same escalators. (Courtesy of the US Farm Security Administration and Office of War Information Collection, LOC Prints and Photographs Division.)

This view up the escalators from the general waiting room toward the shopping arcade reveals how the "moving stairway" designed by the Otis Elevator Company had become such an important fixture. The Pennsylvania Railroad had these installed to replace stairs throughout the station. (Courtesy of the US Farm Security Administration and Office of War Information Collection, LOC Prints and Photographs Division.)

This view into the crowded ladies' waiting room reveals that women and men were no longer segregated, likely a result of overcrowding at the station during the war. In support the war effort, many lights were dimmed or darkened entirely to conserve electricity. (Courtesy of the US Farm Security Administration and Office of War Information Collection, LOC Prints and Photographs Division.)

Large crowds dominate this view of the ladies' waiting room while vending machines and self-service lockers can be seen in the background. These changes to the waiting room and other spaces throughout the station demonstrate its increased use during the war as passengers and amenities were shifted to accommodate the massive influx of service members. (Courtesy of the US Farm Security Administration and Office of War Information Collection, LOC Prints and Photographs Division.)

A woman anxiously waits with her baby on the concourse, perhaps for a relative in the service. A fully staffed nursery with a nurse and matron was established by the USO to offer service members the last private opportunity to meet a spouse before departing for the war. The pink-colored nursery accommodations included four cribs, two high chairs, an electric stove, and a refrigerator. (Courtesy of the US Farm Security Administration and Office of War Information Collection, LOC Prints and Photographs Division.)

A Pennsylvania Railway porter offers assistance to the same woman, which would have been uncommon during the war as many men employed by the railway had been drafted, and women were hired to fill the vacancies. Dressed in uniforms and working directly with passengers, they sold and checked tickets, provided directions, opened gates, and announced train arrivals and departures. (Courtesy of the US Farm Security Administration and Office of War Information Collection, LOC Prints and Photographs Division.)

Bernice Abbott captured this image of passengers waiting for a departure on the concourse in the 1940s. Although unseen here, passengers would have direct access via the concourse to the Pennsylvania Greyhound Terminal adjacent to the station. A joint venture between Greyhound Lines Inc. and the Pennsylvania Railroad, the terminal ensured that the railway could draw additional passengers into the station. Passengers from other nearby bus companies added to the increased business as well. (Courtesy of the Changing New York Collection, Miriam and Ira D. Wallach Art, Prints, and Photographs Division, NYPL.)

Greyhound Lines Inc. hired the renowned theater architect Thomas Lamb (1871–1942) to create a new Art Deco style bus terminal in the 1930s. The brick building, captured here by Bernice Abbott in the 1940s, was adorned with chrome banding, dark blue tiling, and a curvilinear façade, which was accessed from Thirty-Third and Thirty-Fourth Streets between Seventh and Eighth Avenues. The terminal boasted a 200-seat waiting room and could accommodate 5,000 passengers on 275 buses each day. (Courtesy of the Changing New York Collection, Miriam and Ira D. Wallach Art, Prints, and Photographs Division, NYPL.)

The dominance of the automobile has become evident in this image and the next three taken by the architectural photographer Cervin Robinson (born 1928) in May 1962. Looking down Seventh Avenue across the entry façade of Pennsylvania Station, the broad avenue now caters to cars. Many of the elevated rail lines have been demolished in favor of flyovers to accommodate vehicular traffic throughout the city. (Courtesy of the Historic American Buildings Survey, LOC Prints and Photographs Division.)

The rapid rise in personal travel made possible by the automobile and the interstate highway system rendered many railways obsolete by the 1960s. In numerous American cities, urban planners redesigned access almost exclusively for the automobile rather than public transport. As a result, it should not be surprising that the automobile was at the forefront of several of the proposed plans for a new Pennsylvania Station. (Courtesy of the Historic American Buildings Survey, LOC Prints and Photographs Division.)

Beginning in the 1950s, William Zeckendorf (1905–1976), an entrepreneurial developer, proposed constructing a "world trade center" above the tracks between Eighth and Ninth Avenues. His second option entailed a "palace of progress" three times larger than the Empire State Building to be built over Pennsylvania Station itself. The supertall would include permanent displays similar to those in a world's fair and a massive selection of international merchandise. Both projects were scrapped. (Courtesy of the Historic American Buildings Survey, LOC Prints and Photographs Division.)

Another plan considered completely razing Pennsylvania Station for an International style high-rise with several low-rise buildings arranged around an expansive court. An even bolder plan called for partial demolition of the station, leaving the general waiting room and concourse, to create a massive car park. There also were variations of a new Madison Square Garden, which eventually were revised and came to fruition in 1968. (Courtesy of the Historic American Buildings Survey, LOC Prints and Photographs Division.)

This interior view of the concourse from the early 1960s reveals the negative effects of modernization at Pennsylvania Station. The railway, undoubtedly desperate for revenue, permitted unsightly advertising and many businesses to operate on the concourse and throughout the station. In one example, the elegant analog clocks have been draped with signs advertising the 1921-founded Benrus Watch Company, while Coca-Cola has inserted a digital clock at center. (Courtesy of the Historic American Buildings Survey, LOC Prints and Photographs Division.)

The decline of the station is evidenced further by the numerous concession stands, seating areas, storage lockers, vending machines, and popup stores that crowd the concourse in this 1960s image. Many disadvantaged New Yorkers used the concourse as living space. An attempt to clean years of grime from the station surfaces was unsuccessful and actually contributed to its general decay when only areas within reach of the cleaners was remedied. (Courtesy of the Historic American Buildings Survey, LOC Prints and Photographs Division.)

In 1960, Norman McGrath preserved this view of the general waiting room before its impending destruction. Although the splendor of the classical architecture remains, the space has been transformed by a modernist ticket office housing the latest electronic ticketing and reservation system, sales kiosks, shops, and various electronic advertising boards. These changes, intended to revitalize the station, only hindered access, especially when the new ticketing system was plagued with technical problems. (Courtesy of Norman McGrath.)

Further changes were applied to the general waiting room, including the placement of seating moved from the ladies' and men's waiting rooms and the removal of lighting equipment to support electronic advertising. Together, these contributed to a universal clutter. The supplementary waiting rooms had been made redundant to support rows of reservation and ticketing clerks working the new ticket office. This photograph and the next two were taken between 1958 and 1963. (Courtesy of the Historic American Buildings Survey, LOC Prints and Photographs Division.)

Designed by the architect Lester Tichy (1905–1981), the sweeping curvilinear canopy known colloquially as the "clamshell" was suspended by steel cables affixed to the large Corinthian order columns. The contemporary design, unfortunately, was incongruent with the Beaux-Arts station and became a major obstacle between the general waiting room and concourse. Incidentally, the modernist Lester Tichy had been trained by John Russell Pope (1874–1937), a graduate of the École des Beaux Arts and a noted proponent of its namesake style. (Courtesy of the Historic American Buildings Survey, LOC Prints and Photographs Division.)

The Pennsylvania Railroad, unable to form a consensus over the modernization process, only implemented elements of the various proposed plans, namely a new 152-foot-wide steel and aluminum ticket office built at a cost of $2 million. Looking toward the stairs between the general waiting room and shopping arcade, the six-foot-high bronze statue of eighth railway president Samuel Rea, the successor of Alexander Cassatt, stands opposite his predecessor. Today, the statue survives adjacent to Madison Square Garden (1968). (Courtesy of the Historic American Buildings Survey, LOC Prints and Photographs Division.)

Renowned photographer Norman McGrath captured this iconic image of Pennsylvania Station and the next two during its demolition in the early 1960s. Standing on Thirty-Second Street facing the Seventh Avenue façade, he shows the grim news announcing the station redevelopment and construction of Madison Square Garden, the fourth structure to bear this name. The Turner Construction Company, founded in 1902 and specialists in concrete projects, erected the entertainment complex from the station ruins. (Courtesy of Norman McGrath).

In 1964, passengers wait in the original glass-bricked concourse. The concourse was shielded from falling debris during deconstruction, which enabled 250,000 passengers to continue accessing platforms and for 650 trains to remain unimpeded each day. Eventually, the translucent floor was resurfaced, but a few glass bricks remain visible today. (Courtesy of Norman McGrath).

A total of 500 pylons, spaced between three levels of active passenger areas, supported a concrete platform, which protected the concourse and sustained the steel structural framework above for the new entertainment complex. As a result, passengers navigated a labyrinth of dark passages that had become Pennsylvania Station, much like in the previous image, awash in temporary signage and scaffolding. This image, taken in 1963, where the concourse had joined Thirty-Third Street, reveals a heap of smashed Guastavino tiling and Italian travertine marble. (Courtesy of Norman McGrath).

Bedrich Grunzweig provided an alternative concourse view in 1963, revealing the placement of steel structural framework above transiting passengers. Workers were required to deconstruct the old station and erect the new entertainment complex without interrupting commuter traffic. This arrangement was an incredible achievement, reminiscent of demands placed on builders during station construction in the early 20th century, when commercial and residential streets in the Tenderloin neighborhood required unfettered access and the elevated Ninth Avenue Line needed to operate undisturbed. (Courtesy of the Bedrich Grunzweig Photo Archive).

In this image and the next three, Norman McGrath further documents the destruction of Pennsylvania Station during the early 1960s. Looking into a Seventh Avenue carriage portal while sparks fly, workers dismantle the pedestrian bridge that once carried passengers from Thirty-Third Street into the general waiting room. Unfortunately, stone and masonry building materials were incongruent with modernist architectural styles and were not recycled, unlike the example of Madison Square Presbyterian Church. (Courtesy of Norman McGrath).

Workers, surrounded with company signage, break the Milford pink granite façade in 1963. The Lipsett Demolition Company, owned and operated by brothers Morris (1905–1985) and Julius Lipsett (1908–1990), was awarded the Pennsylvania Station wrecking contract. The company had razed many landmarks, including the elevated Third Avenue Line, Singer Manufacturing Company Building, Madison Square Garden (1925), and sections of Grand Central Terminal, the latter for construction of the Pan American World Airways Building in 1959. (Courtesy of Norman McGrath).

A Roman imperial eagle, modeled by Adolph Weinman, has been lowered from its Seventh Avenue perch in 1963. Fortunately, a few eagles were retained for the exterior of Madison Square Garden (1968) and can be seen today at the northern and southern ends of the complex. Although examples were dispersed to other transport centers, including four at Thirtieth Street Station in Philadelphia, much of the ornamentation and building materials were carted to the Meadowlands in New Jersey to be used as fill. (Courtesy of Norman McGrath).

The immense size of the eagles, each 63.5 inches high and 5,700 pounds, can be appreciated as workers carefully lower another survivor in 1963. The failure of government and probably a majority of New Yorkers, although there were some who vociferously protested, to protect or at least repurpose the original Pennsylvania Station was a shameful tragedy. After the displacement of so many immigrant families, the deaths of workers, and the reshaping of an entire neighborhood, it should have endured as a monument to the Gilded Age past. (Courtesy of Norman McGrath).

After deconstruction of Pennsylvania Station and removal of debris was completed by 1965, evidenced by this image Norman McGrath snapped from the Hotel Pennsylvania, pylons and girders were placed above the concrete platform for Madison Square Garden (1968) and two high-rises, One Penn Plaza and Two Penn Plaza. The International style entertainment complex was devised by Charles Luckman (1909–1999), an architect who had designed the John F. Kennedy and Lyndon B. Johnson Space Centers in Cape Canaveral and Houston, respectively, along with Los Angeles International Airport. (Courtesy of Norman McGrath).

Norman McGrath captured this incredible aerial view looking into the center of the massive civil engineering project in 1965. The 20,000-seat circular complex soared 13 stories, and its 425-foot diameter accommodated a 5,000-seat amphitheater, bowling alley, cinema, and exhibition space. The new basement station, with its six main entry points, was fully air-conditioned and equipped with escalators stretching from street to concourse, moving 90,000 passengers each hour. The new station and complex were completed in 1967 and cost $116 million. (Courtesy of Norman McGrath).

Night, the magnificent work of Adolph Weinman, one of four in Tennessee pink marble, has been preserved for future generations in an outdoor garden of another McKim, Mead, and White Beaux-Arts structure, the Brooklyn Museum (1895). For a long time, Brooklyn had been a rival urban center of New York until its union with the city in 1898. In an ironic twist, this iconic fragment of architectural ornamentation was preserved in the leading museum of New York's former adversary. (Courtesy of the Brooklyn Museum).

A second fragment, a truncated Italian travertine marble column from Pennsylvania Station, has been kept in the outdoor garden of the same museum. The Ionic order column base and partial shaft with capital were salvaged from a colonnade in the general waiting room. A few station fragments also survive in a New Jersey Transit storage facility in Newark. (Courtesy of the Brooklyn Museum.)

Five

A New Vision for Pennsylvania Station

Pennsylvania Station continues to operate beneath Madison Square Garden (1968), but only as a faint shadow of the former Beaux-Arts monument designed by McKim, Mead, and White. Electrical failures, flooding, and overcrowding have plagued the station, often resulting in severe delays and cancellations. The entertainment complex above did not fare much better after declining revenues steered it dangerously toward permanent closure in the 1980s. Within 20 years of opening, plans were submitted for the demolition of the arena and the construction of a high-rise office block in its former footprint. Even though the loss of Pennsylvania Station was an epic tragedy, the destruction of its replacement, another masterfully engineered structure, would have been outrageous and wasteful. Fortunately, city and state governments reduced taxes and offered financial subsidies that avoided bankruptcy and spared Madison Square Garden (1968) from the wrecking ball. Recent developments have again pointed toward disaster after proposals surfaced to raze the entertainment complex or retrofit its arena into a new Pennsylvania Station. Both options were vetoed by New York State, but the fate of the complex remains uncertain.

Unfortunately, the Pennsylvania Station scandal and even the Landmarks Preservation Commission cannot stifle the greed common during the Neo Gilded Age of today. The ever-increasing drive to construct supertall luxury apartments has rendered both historic structures, namely the Beaux-Arts Demarest Building (1890), the Beaux-Arts Hotel Pennsylvania (1910), the International style Union Carbide Building (1960), and large-scale structures, including Madison Square Garden (1968), and the International style New York Coliseum (1956), obsolete and expendable. Much like the sweeping changes that ushered in Pennsylvania Station during the Gilded Age and the subsequent reaction when it was deemed too expensive to maintain, the same cycle inevitably will reoccur following the Neo Gilded Age, when residential supertalls will be considered blasé and financially unjustified. Additionally, the astronomical prices for these luxury apartments have forced most of the poor and middle class out of many neighborhoods and emptied whole swaths of the city. After plans were announced to cannibalize the existing General Post Office Building for the Moynihan Train Hall, it was hoped that the legacy of McKim, Mead, and White would be revived. The new station, however, has experienced funding problems and continues to be plagued by delays.

A view of Madison Square Garden (1968) from Eighth Avenue in 2018 after its $11 million renovation in 2011–2013. Quite a departure from the original Madison Square Garden (1879) and second Madison Square Garden (1890) built over Madison Square Park, and even the third Madison Square Garden (1925) on Eighth Avenue between Forty-Ninth and Fiftieth Streets, it generates revenue for the new Pennsylvania Station, now relegated to discrete basement entrances, one of which is barely visible at left. (Photograph by Gregory Bilotto.)

Another image of Madison Square Garden (1968), taken from the corner of Thirty-Third Street and Eighth Avenue in 2019, offers a more complete view of the entertainment venue with its International style tower, Two Penn Plaza. The Beaux-Arts Hotel Pennsylvania, one of the last architectural vestiges of McKim, Mead, and White, now threatened with destruction, can be seen at far left. (Courtesy of Wikimedia Commons.)

A lower-level entry within the station, obscured from daylight and minuscule compared to its architectural antecedent, opens to waiting areas for Amtrak and New Jersey Transit trains. This 2018 image reflects some of the most prevalent problems within the current station, namely a dizzying network of corridors and halls, dimly lit and uncongenial, seemingly built into a basement. (Photograph by Gregory Bilotto.)

The modern shopping hall of Pennsylvania Station is a stark departure from the enormous and naturally lit arcade in the former station. The narrow corridor with artificial lighting ostensibly replicates a train interior, but it cannot support current passenger volume. This image, taken on a weekday afternoon before the evening rush in 2018, already shows overcrowding. (Photograph by Gregory Bilotto.)

This is the ticket hall in 2018, with passengers of the Long Island Railroad waiting in front of the new digital display board. Tight, crowded, and dark when compared to the general waiting room and ticket hall of the former station, passengers often lament the congestion and absence of any seating. The 1960s-era split-flap display, an electromechanical board with fixed letters and digits, was replaced in January 2017 by Amtrak. (Photograph by Gregory Bilotto.)

At the end of the shopping hall, the legacy of the former Pennsylvania Station endures through five artworks created in 1994 by Andrew Leicester (born 1948). Produced from enamel, porcelain, and terra-cotta, the *Ghost Series* includes several scenes reminiscent of the lost railway station, including an interpretation of *Day* and *Night* in a 500-square-foot mural, seen here in 2018. The sculptural arrangement that once graced all four entrances of the station was reproduced in a unique life-sized form. (Photograph by Gregory Bilotto.)

The Corinthian order façade of the General Post Office Building, renamed after the postmaster general James A. Farley (1888–1976) in 1982, remains mostly true to its original 1912 design, except for the West Annex. The impressive colonnade, rich with architectural detail, provides a semblance of the former grandeur that Pennsylvania Station once commanded. In this image, and the next three, taken in 2018, the post office survives as the most original and complete remnant of the former Pennsylvania Station. (Photograph by Gregory Bilotto.)

Entering the interior retail gallery from the steps on Eighth Avenue, the ornate ceiling, alternating Corinthian triangular and lunette pediments, and even the original lighting scheme have been retained. Although modern furniture crowds the lobby and most of the retail windows have been shuttered, the classical design advanced by McKim, Mead, and White can be fully appreciated. (Photograph by Gregory Bilotto.)

Looking closer at the ceiling, a pair of emblems representing two of the Western powers in 1912, the United Kingdom and the French Third Republic, are visible. The others, including the Austro-Hungarian, German, and Russian Empires, the Kingdoms of Belgium, Italy, the Netherlands, and Spain, and the United States, continue throughout the gallery. The architects embraced Western countries and excluded the Ottoman and Japanese Empires because only the West was equated to the classical past, a recurring theme during the Age of Colonialism. (Photograph by Gregory Bilotto.)

A view into the pavilion framing the entry on Eighth Avenue and Thirty-First Street offers a glimpse of the magnificent classical decoration selected and applied by McKim, Mead, and White for the General Post Office Building. Many of the motifs were standard on Roman public architecture, especially the egg-and-dart theme and the large rosette, which also adorned Pennsylvania Station. (Photograph by Gregory Bilotto.)

The Hotel Pennsylvania, at 401 Seventh Avenue, was completed in 1919 for the Pennsylvania Railroad. Intended as a luxurious accommodation for transiting passengers, it welcomed Duke Ellington and Count Basie, among others, to Café Rouge, a nightclub popular during the 1930s and early 1940s with Big Band music. Many Beaux-Arts details are recognizable in the hotel façade, seen here in 2018, including balustrades, dentilled cornices, an Ionic columned portico, Ionic pilasters, Roman triangular pediments, and abundant fenestration. (Photograph by Gregory Bilotto.)

The hotel, still operational when this photograph was taken in 2018, continues to be threatened with destruction. The initial purchase of the building in 1997 by Vornado Realty Trust, a real estate investment trust, resulted in numerous demolition proposals over the last 20 years in favor of constructing a luxury rental high-rise. More recently, in February 2020, plans to raze the hotel were renewed with a cantilevered platform supertall set to be its replacement. Unfortunately, applications to the New York City Landmarks Preservation Commission have proven unsuccessful. (Photograph by Gregory Bilotto.)

Another remnant from Pennsylvania Station, the New York Terminal Service Plant at 250 West Thirty-First Street, was erected in 1908 by McKim, Mead, and White. The Beaux-Arts style structure, constructed from bricks with a granite façade, was adorned with Ionic pilasters, multi-layered pediments, and numerous symmetrical windows. The latter, unusual for an industrial building, was intended to balance aesthetics with utility. Here, the plant is seen in the 1990s before the dual smokestacks were demolished. (Courtesy of the Historic American Buildings Survey, LOC Prints and Photographs Division.)

This interior view of the power plant, also from the 1990s, shows the remnants of a turbine needed to generate electricity for the railway station. Additionally, the plant supplied compressed air for braking and signaling, elevator hydraulics, heating, and refrigeration, and facilitated waste incineration. The plant remains derelict today and faces demolition. It is one of the few remaining structures from the original station and would be better served as new offices or retail space. (Courtesy of the Historic American Buildings Survey, LOC Prints and Photographs Division.)

In this 2018 photograph, the banner fastened to the construction façade of the James A. Farley Post Office announces the future Moynihan Train Hall. Work commenced in 2016 after New York State implemented a scheme for an improved and modernized Pennsylvania Station. Named after US Senator Daniel Patrick Moynihan (1927–2003), who represented New York and was a staunch advocate for the revitalization of Pennsylvania Station, the post office will be shuttered and converted into a new station for the Long Island Railroad and Amtrak. (Photograph by Gregory Bilotto.)

This view of Madison Square Garden (1968) with Two Penn Plaza and the James A. Farley Post Office, soon to be converted into the Moynihan Train Hall, was captured from the Empire State Building in 2008. The glazed steel and aluminum high-rise at right, One Penn Plaza, was built in 1972. The sleek office tower at 234 West Thirty-Fourth Street was designed by the firm Kahn and Jacobs in the International style and has remained the tallest of the 1960s redevelopment of Pennsylvania Station. (Courtesy of Wikimedia Commons.)

Skidmore, Owings, and Merrill, a Chicago based architecture firm founded in the 1930s, was selected to design the future Pennsylvania Station rebranded as Moynihan Train Hall. The firm, responsible for numerous landmark projects—including the Willis (Sears) Tower (1973) and One World Trade Center (2013)—released this rendering of the new transport hub. Looking toward the West Annex on Eighth Avenue, the mail sorting facility has been transformed into an imposing railway station. (Courtesy of the Empire State Development Corporation.)

This rendering of Moynihan Train Hall shows 13 supertalls and high-rises to be constructed over a platform covering Hudson Yards, a 28-acre storage area for Pennsylvania Station trains, with an additional three buildings adjacent to the site. The cluster of modernist structures will provide office, residential, and retail options, along with a performing arts center. The new station would preserve the architectural order devised by McKim, Mead, and White, while integrating green spaces at street level and along the rooflines. (Courtesy of the Empire State Development Corporation.)

In this cross-sectional rendering, the central space of the post office is transformed into a multilevel atrium culminating in a 95-foot-high vaulted and glazed ceiling resting on the original trusses. Long Island Railroad and Amtrak services will share nine platforms and 17 tracks accessed by 11 escalators and seven elevators. The train hall would span 255,000 square feet, which would be larger than the Grand Central Terminal concourse. The Eighth Avenue subway would be directly accessible from the new station. (Courtesy of the Empire State Development Corporation.)

A final rendering provides a visualization of the future railway station with digital signs and timetables. The total cost of the project, divided into two phases, is estimated at $1.6 billion and will be apportioned between Amtrak, the Metropolitan Transportation Authority, New York State, and other stakeholders. Beset with many delays, it is projected to be completed in 2021. (Courtesy of the Empire State Development Corporation.)

Bibliography

Bilotto, Gregory, and Frank DiLorenzo. *Building Grand Central Terminal*. Charleston, SC: Arcadia Publishing, 2017.

Broderick, Mosette. *Triumvirate McKim, Mead, and White: Art, Architecture, Scandal, and Class in America's Gilded Age*. New York, NY: Alfred A. Knopf, 2010.

Crain, Esther. *The Gilded Age in New York: 1870–1910*. New York, NY: Black Dog and Leventhal Publishers, 2016.

Diehl, Lorraine B. *The Late, Great Pennsylvania Station*. New York, NY: Four Walls Eight Windows, 1985.

Greenhalgh, Paul. *Ephemeral Vistas: The Expositions Universelles, Great Exhibitions, and World's Fairs, 1851–1939*. Manchester, UK: Manchester University Press, 1988.

Kaplan, Paul M. *New York's Original Penn Station: The Rise and Tragic Fall of an American Landmark*. Charleston, SC: The History Press, 2019.

Mathieu, Caroline. *Musée d'Orsay: Spirit of Place*. Paris, FR: Nouvelles Éditions Scala, 2013.

McKim, Charles Follen, William Rutherford Mead, Stanford White, and Richard Guy Wilson. *McKim, Mead, and White: Selected Works 1879–1915*. New York, NY: Princeton Architectural Press, 2018.

Middleton, William D. *Manhattan Gateway: New York's Pennsylvania Station*. Waukesha, WI: Kalmbach Publishing Co., 1996.

Ochsendorf, John. *Guastavino Vaulting: The Art of the Structural Tile*. New York, NY: Princeton Architectural Press, 2010.

Parissien, Steven. *Pennsylvania Station: McKim, Mead, and White*. London, UK: Phaidon Press Ltd., 1996.

Pennsylvania Station in New York City. 1910. Reprint, New York, NY: Metroray Studio, 2017.

Reed, Henry Hope, and Edmund V. Gillion Jr. *Beaux Arts Architecture in New York: A Photographic Guide*. New York, NY: Dover Publications Inc., 1988.

Stern, Robert A.M., Thomas Mellins, and David Fishman. *New York 1880: Architecture and Urbanism in the Gilded Age*. New York, NY: Monacelli Press, 1999.

———. *New York 1960: Architecture and Urbanism between the Second World War and Bicentennial*. New York, NY: Monacelli Press, 1995.

Stern, Robert A.M., Gregory Gilmartin, and John Massengale. *New York 1900: Metropolitan Architecture and Urbanism 1890–1915*. Rizzoli International Publications, 1995.

White, Samuel G. and Elizabeth. *McKim, Mead, and White: The Masterworks*. New York, NY: Rizzoli International Publications, 2003.

———. *Stanford White: Architect*. New York, NY: Rizzoli International Publications, 2008.

White, Samuel G. *Stanford White in Detail*. New York, NY: Monacelli Press, 2020.

Index

MADE IN THE
USA